The Business Owner's ESSENTIAL GUIDE TO I.T. AND ALL THINGS DIGITAL

VERSION 2.0

Published by CelebrityPress®, Orlando, FL.

CelebrityPress® is a registered trademark.

Printed in the United States of America.

ISBN: 978-0-9907064-2-7
LCCN: 2014950915

This publication is designed to provide accurate and authoritative information with regard to the subject matter covered. It is sold with the understanding that the publisher is not engaged in rendering legal, accounting, or other professional advice. If legal advice or other expert assistance is required, the services of a competent professional should be sought. The opinions expressed by the authors in this book are not endorsed by Celebrity Press® and are the sole responsibility of the authors rendering the opinion.

Most CelebrityPress® titles are available at special quantity discounts for bulk purchases for sales promotions, premiums, fundraising, and educational use. Special versions or book excerpts can also be created to fit specific needs.

For more information, please write:
CelebrityPress®
520 N. Orlando Ave, #2
Winter Park, FL 32789
or call 1.877.261.4930

Visit us online at: www.CelebrityPressPublishing.com

The Business Owner's ESSENTIAL GUIDE TO I.T. AND ALL THINGS DIGITAL

VERSION 2.0

CELEBRITY PRESS®
Winter Park, Florida

CONTENTS

FOREWORD

BY ROBIN ROBINS

*Wealth continually grows from multiplying existing resources
using existing technologies.*
~ Paul Zane Pilzer,
American Economist, Professor and Entrepreneur

If you're over the age of 35 reading this book, chances are you
remember a time when the latest car phone technology consisted of
a 10-pound brick you carried around, complete with an antenna and
a corded handset that plugged into your car's cigarette lighter. Mine
even had a shoulder strap. You might also recall how cool you felt
when you bought your first Sony Walkman or CD player and how
you had to unplug the phone line to get access to AOL via your phone
modem.

Although this seems like YEARS ago, it's only been a blip on the
timeline of life. And today, new and disruptive breakthroughs in
technology are literally changing the way we work, service our
customers, communicate with others and run our businesses.

We've seen the demise of public pay phones, DVD rental stores and
even bookstores with the omnipresence of fast Internet connections
and the proliferation of cheap devices. We no longer need to leave the
house to buy a car or groceries. And business is conducted nationally
and globally with people we've never met, merchandise we've never
touched, and in online stores we've never walked into.

These technological advances HAVE made starting, growing and running a business infinitely easier. With a few clicks we can send e-mail or text messages to millions of people instantaneously at a fraction of the cost of other media. Finding detailed information on our customers, competition and market trends can be found in minutes for free. And the massive amounts of information required to operate a business – from accounting, client data, inventory, payroll, work products and more – is all easily stored, searched and available quickly and easily, thanks to the ever-growing software systems and electronic storage of data online.

But this convenience has also come with a price. New technologies (and our dependence on them), have introduced a number of new challenges and threats that, if not addressed, can bring even the most successful company to its knees in a moment. Which is why I was so honored and excited to write the foreword of this book.

For years, I've acted as a marketing and business consultant to thousands of IT services companies, giving me a unique insight into this group of smart, hard-working men and women who keep the millions of small business owners around the world up and running.

It is my experience that these are some of the most under-utilized and under-appreciated group of professionals serving small business owners today. With new technologies coming online daily and millions of new threats cropping up moment-by-moment, they have the unique and massively difficult job of staying on top of it all – just to make sure your Internet doesn't go down, your e-mail is always available and your systems are always running.

They spend their days constantly fighting a never-ending stream of fresh, new, problems, attempting to make multiple-disconnected software systems and applications all play together "nice," so you, as the user, experience zero delays, problems or downtime – all on a shoestring budget and a limited timeframe. And when they're successful overcoming this incredibly difficult task, they often don't get the "thanks" they deserve.

Technology is a vastly powerful tool; but if you don't know how to apply it properly, you could end up like the Indian chief who, when given a brand new car, hitched up his trusted old team of donkeys to pull it along as his new mode of transportation, grossly ignorant of the power he had available to him with a single turn of a key. This book and the IT consultants you're about to meet, hold that key.

Each and every one of the professionals you're about to meet in this book exemplifies leadership, business savvy, dedication, professionalism and a passion for excellence. Each of them holds several keys to making your business more secure, more profitable, more successful and more efficient. I would strongly encourage you to take to heart their advice and words of wisdom.

CHAPTER 1

HOW YOUR BUSINESS CAN BENEFIT FROM SOCIAL MEDIA

BY ERIC TOWNSEND

When you think about the advent of web-based media, in the beginning a business only had their company web page to communicate with their customers. Then, as social networks came on the scene and began to grow and evolve, we saw other opportunities for a business to communicate with customers and potential customers.

We all know Facebook began in a college dorm room as a way for students to share information about themselves and the various happenings in their life. Since its public release, the site has evolved to include business pages—giving businesses an expanded reach. Businesses began to utilize Facebook for everything from telling others about their products and services to informing them of what the company was doing in the community, and to even recruiting new talent.

Twitter and LinkedIn followed Facebook, producing additional information channels for individuals as well as for companies. Many small and medium-sized businesses initially used micro-messages on Twitter simply as a way to build their brand, broadcasting messages to all who "followed" them. But Twitter has evolved and smart companies now use it to listen and converse with their customers.

17

LinkedIn is a social network focused solely on work. Employees and executives have LinkedIn profiles where they share information, while companies use LinkedIn Groups or company profiles to showcase business information. Think of it like a job fair or networking mixer on steroids. Pinterest and Instagram have been the newest revolution being adapted for business use. Businesses are realizing there is an important segment of their market that is very visual and these platforms allow them to communicate creatively with this group. This is one of the fastest growing social media platforms for businesses today, because they recognize it as a unique and very visual way to get their brand in front of a growing segment of potential customers. In Instagram, for example, a company may post a picture of one of their products with a related caption and hashtags. In fact, there are an estimated 20 billion photos shared by businesses every month on Instagram—that's 60 million photos per day.[i]

YouTube has also become a phenomenon, and is the second largest search engine[ii] used today. Many people are searching for new content via video and YouTube is their main search choice. Businesses take advantage of this medium by posting rich content videos as another means to connect with their current customers as well as with potential clientele. Whether you are showcasing a new product or showing customers how to enable a product feature, YouTube let's your customers feel like you are right in the room with them.

While these numbers change daily, a statistical snapshot of daily use puts into perspective the power of social media. In 2012, the following occurred on a **daily** basis:

- Enough information is consumed by Internet traffic to fill 168 million DVD's
- 2 million blog posts are written

---

i. http://business.instagram.com/

ii. http://www.mushroomnetworks.com/infographics/youtube — the-2nd-largest-search-engine-infographic

- 172 million different people visit Facebook
- 40 million different people visit Twitter
- 22 million different people visit LinkedIn
- 17 million different people visit Pinterest
- 4.7 billion minutes are spent on Facebook
- 532 million statuses are updated
- 250 million photos are uploaded to Facebook
- 864,000 hours of video are uploaded to YouTube[iii]

SOCIAL MEDIA AND BUSINESS

Social media is constantly changing and shifting in that it is becoming broader in scope, and much more robust. There are continuous updates being made enabling businesses to take advantage of very powerful tools. Smart business owners and leaders realize it isn't enough to just put content on social media platforms. But, there must be a distinct strategy to how they are using social media.

Not only have the social media platforms gone through an evolutionary process, but the way we view these platforms has also experienced a tremendous transformation. In the beginning, social media was viewed from the standard desk top computer. However, now we are seeing a surge in tablet use and other mobile devices such as smartphones – which people can carry with them wherever they go – so they can be constantly connected.

Business-class 2-in-1 devices are also changing our interactions—these can be utilized as a notebook with a keyboard, or used as a tablet simply by flipping the screen. Today individuals are going everywhere and anywhere with their business-class tablets, their 2-in-1s and mobile devices, capturing and consuming content literally around

---

iii. "A Day In the Life of the Internet."
http://mashable.com/2012/03/06/one-day-internet-data-traffic

the clock and around the world. This makes the need to connect with customers—when and where they want—even more crucial. Your customers are already online looking for you – you need to be there waiting.

THREE KEY WAYS TO GAIN MORE VALUE FROM YOUR SOCIAL MEDIA ACTIVITIES

I. Start Creating Customer Conversations, Not More Collateral

From customer support to customer acquisition to building long-term relationships, social media for business is designed, in part, for conversation. Let's be clear. Social media is not advertising, but rather involves information about what your company is doing, what your staff is learning about, that will positively impact customer service, or anything that may potentially be of interest to your customer base and draw attention to your brand. Businesses with a defined social media strategy understand there is a difference between listening and broadcasting. With social media, you have the opportunity to really listen to what your customers are saying. By listening you can actually find out what is important to your customers and then gear marketing, promotions, and future social conversations to address your customers concerns and needs. You don't have to wait for weeks to evaluate the effect of your message. In some instances you will be able to gauge its effectiveness by the real time responses you receive and can adjust your message "on the fly." By taking this approach, you aren't a marketing hammer, hitting them over the head with content. Rather, you are listening and communicating much as you would in a face-to-face encounter.

Social media allows companies to hear from their customers without having to form focus groups or collect customer feedback in some other form. With social media, you have direct access to your customers and you can immediately gauge their response to your messages, products and services, thereby enabling you to be more competitive and successful. In the past, a customer may have sent a letter of complaint or concern to a business by US Mail. It may have taken a few days for that piece of mail to be routed to the appropriate person, and then the letter might have sat on a desk for several days. By the time a response was formulated, a couple of weeks might have passed. However, with social media, a concern can be expressed and "heard" by your company immediately. Smart companies will offer a response very quickly to their customer.

Share buttons are very helpful to businesses and your customers should be encouraged to use them regularly. Part of your social media strategy should be to post content that is so creative and intriguing that the recipient will want to share that content with their friends and connections. When that happens, your content exposure then grows exponentially and your reach becomes far greater than the limitations of your social media followers. By sharing your content, your customers are actually advertising for you and it becomes just like "word of mouth" marketing. You're customers become a raving fan for you!

Interestingly, only 47% of small and medium-sized businesses using social media have increased their advertising spending.[iv] That's because social media lends itself to organic lead generation that doesn't usually have any associated cost. Social media also allows a business to advertise in a very focused manner on a specific market so they can zero-in on that market with precision.

II. Gather Your Employees Around the Digital Water Cooler

Social media isn't just for communicating with your external customers. There is great value in utilizing this methodology to also communicate with your employees and develop those relationships within the walls of the corporation.

A lot of companies are utilizing social media when bringing on new employees, training, and communicating new initiatives. While HR continues to consider onboarding in their realm, time to productivity is a management concern. Social media joins these two departments

---

iv. "How SMBs Use Social Media: 15 New Stats You Should Know." http://blog.hubspot.com/marketing/stats-smb-social-media-list

together, helping accelerate knowledge transfer and employee engagement. A perfect example is "gameifying" onboarding tasks such as training and enrolling in benefits. With a social platform in place, you can award new employees points or badges as they accomplish a set of activities. This is crucial, especially when you consider that 22% of employee turnover happens in the first 45 days.[v]

As you can imagine, the potential list of uses for this social communication is almost endless. With collaborative platforms such as Yammer or Jive, employees and their company can easily connect and communicate. Social platforms at work connect the right people to the right information, enabling them to share across teams and organize around projects, improving productivity, communication, and employee engagement.

Regardless of the size of your business, the various departments may not work closely together. The sales team, for example, may not have interaction with the customer service team or the operations team. But by having an internal social media platform in place, you are able to bring departments and people together to enhance communication, collaboration and contribute to the overall morale of the company. Social media within a company can enable you to have the old "water cooler" experience. There was a time when people would literally stand around the water cooler and talk. While that may seem old fashioned, there was a lot of information shared. Social media, in a sense, gives people the same type of experience. It's simply another way to build community and employee engagement. We all know that if employees are not engaged in a company, they are not happy employees.

Engaged employees feel like they are part of a community and they enjoy direct communication within all levels of their company. You might utilize social media to solve a problem and engage employees at the same time. For example, if your company were experiencing a downturn in customer satisfaction, you could post the issue on an

---

v. "Help New Hires Succeed: Beat the Statistics." http://www.hr.com/en/app/blog/2007/05/help-new-hires-succeed-beat-the-statistics_f24qxvt5.html

internal message board asking everyone within the company to offer their ideas as to how the problem could be addressed. This type of action lets employees know their opinion is valued, it allows for collaborative thinking (one thought may prompt additional thoughts by others), and it can help you quickly resolve an issue.

III. It's Your Decision: Build Your Brand or Increase Demand

Of course, you still must build your brand and sell your products or services, and social media helps with both these tasks. There are no geographic boundaries when it comes to social media. You are able to reach more customers and potential customers by strategically employing numerous social media platforms.

Positioning your company – by which I mean building your brand – or increasing demand for your products and services is no longer limited to a call center campaign or an email blast, a brochure or a billboard, a radio spot or a web banner. With social media, you are now able to engage customers through targeted Facebook campaigns, attract them through YouTube videos, talk to them on Twitter, or connect with them through another social media platform. When conversations begin in response to your social media efforts, your exposure increases tremendously – which leads to more brand impressions and greater demand for your offerings.

Consider how Oreo took advantage of the blackout that occurred during the 2013 Super Bowl.[vi] A savvy social media team capitalized on the power outage, tweeting, "You can still dunk in the dark." The tweet delivered immediate, quantifiable brand results: 15,811 retweets and an increase in 2,200 followers. Talk about entering into the customer conversation and positioning your brand in a relevant way.

READY, SET, POST!

When considering social media, don't get hung up on the word "media." The world has always been social – and that's all you're

---

vi. "Beyond Super Bowl Stunt, Oreo Finds New Voice In Social Media."
   http://adage.com/article/special-report-digital-alist-2013/ad-age-s-digital-a-list-oreo/239942/

doing with Twitter or Facebook or LinkedIn or any of the other social channels. It's listening and talking, sharing information rather than showcasing products. Also, try not to be overwhelmed by the number of social platforms available! You don't need to be on every one of them. Choose the two that feel most natural to you and then spend 15 minutes a day and "watch" what's happening first. See how other companies similar to yours are using Pinterest or Instagram or Twitter. Then begin engaging – whether internally with employees or externally with customers. It really doesn't have to take a lot of time.

In addition, find a few employees who are social media advocates – and remember, these may not be the youngest employees in your organization. A growing number of Boomers and Gen Xers also see the value in social media. Finally, be authentic, relevant, and consistent. You'll be engaging sooner than you think.

About Eric

A technology marketing executive with a history of applying tech innovations to emerging business trends, resulting in breakthrough increases in sales and margins, Eric D. Townsend has the ability to take a concept from ideation to creation through execution.

For nearly two decades, Eric's work has promoted the practical, positive impact of technologies across the computing spectrum—from hardware to software to services. He has worked with various companies in multiple industries to grow technology usages that build business and increase profitability. This includes extensive work and significant initiatives in the healthcare, retail and manufacturing industries.

Eric is currently the director of SMB Marketing for North America for Intel Corporation and works closely with technology vendors and IT service providers serving the small and medium business market. As managed IT services have matured over the last 10 years, Eric has been a leader in the adoption of advanced remote services and emerging tools, working with over 300 IT service providers and all major vendors of IT hardware. His focus on growing business through the intelligent evolution of IT processes— as opposed to technology for technology's sake—has attracted a strong network of fellow travelers and helped forge multi-party initiatives that deliver broad and sustainable value. In addition, Eric helps MSPs and IT consultants reach customers easily and effectively using a mix of social media and content marketing to build brand and increase demand. Eric has a keen understanding of how social media is changing every industry and how businesses should be empowered by this rather than afraid of it.

Eric is also deeply committed to supporting local community efforts and helping people in need. For 6 years, he has volunteered his time weekly at Phoenix Children's Hospital, which provides world-class care to children throughout the state and region. He also works regularly on various U.S. and international housing projects through Habitat for Humanity, including builds in Fiji, New Zealand, South Africa, and Trinidad, as well as domestically in Arizona.

Connect with Eric D. Townsend on LinkedIn.

CHAPTER 2

BYOD: THE ADVANTAGES, RISKS AND EFFECTIVE MANAGEMENT OF MOBILE DEVICES IN THE CORPORATE WORLD

BY ALEX ROMP

By simple definition, BYOD (Bring Your Own Device) refers to the policy of allowing employees to bring their personal mobile devices (laptops, tablets, smartphones, etc.) to the workplace, and to use these devices to access and work on privileged company information and apps. A truly global phenomenon, it is estimated that about 75 percent of employees in high-growth markets like Brazil and Russia and 44 percent in developed markets are already engaged in this practice, which is generally seen as helping employees become more productive in their work.

For a majority of organizations, BYOD can be as simple as taking business calls on a personal cell phone, but in general, it's about allowing people to do their PIM (Personal Information Management) on their phone, including, of course, business related email. Everyone seems to want and use it. People are sending their company documents to their personal email and opening it at home – on the same devices that their kids may use for other reasons. And the files being opened keep getting bigger. One of my clients recently tried to email a 200 MB file.

Most people are so enthralled with the convenience of taking their work wherever they go that they don't seem to think of the consequences of security risks involved in what they are doing. So when they synchronize a Dropbox file to a home computer, they're not thinking about the malware that may be lurking there. Most malware is financially motivated, where hackers are looking for financial data, credit card numbers, Social Security numbers, bank accounts, etc.

I don't want to fill this chapter with too much info on viruses and malware, but I think it's important to mention it upfront because understanding the risks will help ensure a positive and productive BYOD experience. Many of the largest security breaches that happen occur because people install programs on their office computers, then connect their home computers to those without the knowledge of the company or their IT department. In CompTIA's most recent mobility survey, they estimate that 64 percent of companies allow or mandate employees to use their mobile devices to increase productivity, but 12 percent are said to accept it only because it is too hard to keep employees from doing it. One of the growing alternatives to BYOD is COPE (gotta love those IT-world acronyms!), which means Company Owned, Personally Enabled devices. With COPE, the company gives an iPhone or similar device to their employees, but they control the security on it.

WHY BYOD?

In today's world, the slickest new toys and gadgets are being designed for end users, which translates to the "consumerization of IT." These devices are designed to make consumers want to buy them. Laptops were part of the initial push into the ability for people to work remotely. But they could still largely be controlled and secured by IT departments, which could install management technology and utilize security features built into the systems. But with few exceptions, manufacturers are not developing smartphones with company security in mind – and their devices extend mobility far beyond that of laptops.

On the risk side, IT departments cannot as easily standardize basic functions and security. But on the plus side, there are great cost savings since employees provide the devices – and there is the potential for a great increase in productivity since employees can now work 24/7 from anywhere. Of course, this could be offset by the costs associated with management of the devices. A data breach situation might occur if you leave your laptop or phone with sensitive data – let's say a spreadsheet with hundreds of Social Security numbers - in a cab, and the devices were not properly secured. Or you could get sensitive data captured by malware at any time. So any productivity gains could be offset by the resources and new software it takes to mop this up.

It's important to weigh the pros and cons when considering incorporating BYOD into your business structure. Another big "pro" is employee satisfaction, since they no longer need to carry multiple devices and they can choose the "flavor" they prefer when it comes to mobile device vendors (Apple vs. Android, phone vs. tablet). The Gartner Group, a major research company, predicts that four in ten organizations will rely exclusively on BYOD by 2016. That would not surprise me at all.

CALCULATING THE RISKS

As we've established, a lost, stolen or malware-infected device can pose a major risk for companies. You can mitigate the damages of a lost or stolen device by having a strictly enforced password on a device, or through a mechanism where the device wipes itself, or "self destructs" if you enter the wrong one ten times. If you hook the phone up to an email server, you can require the device to have a passcode setup before it synchronizes your email. Another interesting emerging technology that deals with this problem is the "walled garden" approach (implemented by such systems as "AirWatch" and Samsung's "Knox"), which isolates company data. Instead of allowing your phone's native email apps to sync with corporate servers, they have their own application for such access. The advantage of this is that if your IT department has to wipe the device of an employee, they can simply wipe the corporate data and leave the personal data intact.

This allows the IT department to enforce stronger security to access corporate data if the device owner doesn't want to deal with passcodes just to access their personal information.

In discussing malware, a few stats are worth considering: 52 percent of mobile devices in the U.S. are Android-based, and nearly 80 percent worldwide. This is significant because compared to Apple platforms, Androids are generally more susceptible to malware because they run on a more open system. Also, 75 percent of attacks on these devices are targets of opportunity, rather than attacks directed at a person or organization. You don't have to be targeted, you just have to be vulnerable. Sometimes these attacks simply happen when you download the wrong app or click an email link you should not have. Or it can happen when you loan your young child your tablet and he or she innocently clicks on the wrong thing. Those who write malware programs are not kids in their parents' basement, but opportunists creating viruses specifically with a Return on Investment (ROI) in mind.

Data breaches can lead to severe penalties when they fall under the domain of such organizations and legislations like HIPAA (The Health Insurance Portability and Accountability Act), The PCI (Payment Card Industry) Data Security Standard and Sarbanes-Oxley (the federal law that set new or enhanced standards for all U.S. public company boards, management and public accounting firms). Losses have to be reported, even across state lines, and a company is required in some cases to put out a press release if more than 500 people's information could have been compromised.

No company wants to see themselves on the news because something was stolen and someone now has access to sensitive digital data. Data loss/leak can involve anything from corporate data to trade secrets and confidential employee information. When customer data is lost, mandatory reporting to the government could be required. HIPAA also requires mandatory reporting on the loss of PHI (Personal Health Information).

MANAGEMENT OF DEVICES

One of the most common ways companies manage the thousands of devices their employees use is with MDM, or Mobile Device Management software. The main advantage of this is that it allows all the devices to be managed from a central location. It secures, monitors, manages and supports mobile devices, and its functionality typically includes over the air distribution of apps, security and configuration settings such as wireless networks and email servers. MDM software can apply to both company and employee-owned devices. Consumer demand for BYOD is now requiring a greater effort for MDM and increased security for both the devices and the enterprise they connect to.

MDM allows for a fast rollout of policies, apps and settings. IT can look at a single pane of glass (viewing all the devices at once) and catch one weak spot on the pane, so to speak. We can use the interface to create security policies that require the phone to go to sleep after five minutes of inactivity. Or we can create an alpha-numeric password and a mechanism by which if you get the password wrong a certain number of times, it will wipe itself. Companies can even create an internal app store through their MDM software where employees can go to download secured, company-only apps for their devices.

Most MDM software has a basic set of capabilities that don't differ much between vendors. In addition to the aforementioned "device wipe," these include: Inventory, email configuration and updates, Wi-Fi settings, password policies, a lock screen policy, an application whitelist/blacklist, and controlling feature access (which can block the use of a camera or app store).

Of course, many employees have bones to pick with the use of MDM. They generally don't want their company's IT department forcing them to have a password, nor do they want their bosses to have access to the personal information on the phone. This is a bigger problem than most realize. Tech industry research giant Gartner predicts that by 2017, one in five BYOD programs will fail due to overly-restrictive MDM policies. Employees expect to enjoy freedom on a device that they own. When it begins to resemble a typical IT locked-down device, they no longer like it. So it's a very delicate balancing act, with such issues often best solved by the "walled garden" approach through the use of some software suites.

Those disgruntled by MDM will be happy to know that some of the tougher security features are very limited by device vendors not allowing certain settings from software. For instance, all mobile applications run in a "sandbox" which prevents them from accessing anything they weren't specifically granted access to from the beginning. MDM vendors also have to work within the restrictions of the mobile operating system. They can't jailbreak or root your phone. MDM software vendors can only work with the tools given to them by phone vendors.

SOFTWARE SUITES

This brings us to Software Suites - which are like MDM on steroids. With traditional BYOD, you hook your phone and its mail program to the company's email server. This is different because the software package itself has its own email and contact manager – and that is simply installed on the phone. It doesn't allow the native Apple or Android mail app to talk to the server, it only allows a secure program to communicate. In other words, it offers access to company data from within its own app suite rather than just pushing the settings to the native phone applications like email, contacts, etc.

Of course, there are issues, like a much higher cost per seat than basic MDM software platforms. And users may not like the separate email application if they're used to the native phone email apps. But as with everything else related to BYOD, a bigger concern is security. ActiveSync is the protocol that synchronizes email to an Exchange server, and it has some very basic security policies available. One is a lock/lockout/wipe policy, which small businesses with Exchange servers should have to lock the phone for protection when their employees are using it. Another is the ActiveSync quarantine function, which sets a limit on which users/devices can sync with your mail server. By default, anybody who knows the web address and the email password can set up a new device, even if it's not the email account owner. With the quarantine, when a device is configured, no one can access mail on it until the company's IT department specifically approves it.

SETTING STANDARD BYOD POLICIES

In light of all of the issues addressed in this chapter, it's not only highly recommended but common sense to have policies in place regarding BYOD – even if your company has formally banned it. You have to make sure everyone is on the same page and knows how you are dealing with potential problems. These policies should be openly discussed and routinely revisited – not simply tucked away in a policy manual. The information that is "out there" with BYOD is too vital.

The main issues to consider, beyond whether to allow BYOD in the first place, is addressing what happens when an employee leaves. Should the IT department remove all corporate data from their device? Or should the entire phone be wiped? My company recommends a policy that says when an employee leaves, in the absence of a "walled garden," that he or she brings IT the phone to remove accounts that allow access to company data, but leaves everything else intact. And if the departing employee doesn't agree to let IT delete the sensitive data, then IT from a legal standpoint has the right to wipe the phone— based on the acceptable use policy that the company should have in place and the employee agreed to.

Another obvious area of policy is deciding what you want your employees doing outside of work on their own devices. Can they make phone calls? Check and send corporate emails? Have access to corporate documents and applications? Will they have remote access to corporate computers? Your policy needs to dictate what is specifically allowed, based on the increased productivity vs. risk paradigm. You should evaluate the risks of breach in any of the above areas. So you have to decide what is most important for your company. The risks may outweigh the benefits for some organizations where security is dictated by regulatory bodies. Some companies also have policies in place that protect them against having to later pay overtime, accomplishing this by shutting down access after business hours or restricting remote access to exempt employees. It's important for companies to walk the line between security and usability.

If you're considering BYOD or just recently implemented it, start by making sure that employees with an Android device have antivirus software installed. Unfortunately, to date there is no approved antivirus program for iPhones, so at the very least make sure they have the "Find my iPhone" app...and then you can upgrade with more sophisticated anti-theft and tracking software later.

About Alex

Alex Romp is the President of Artech Solutions, Inc., an IT consulting firm located in West Des Moines, Iowa, that helps local businesses solve IT challenges and make their infrastructure support their businesses. Like many other Managed Service Providers, Artech began as a simple break-fix company, but Alex quickly realized how the Managed Service model was the future because of the great benefits it provided to his clients.

Artech's focus is primarily on managed IT services and network consulting. It has always been a service company first and foremost, and didn't push product sales to its clients unless it was something that would benefit the client. Alex puts his customers and employees first and he teaches his employees that customer service is the primary function of their jobs. Too often IT people are seen as arrogant individuals who talk down to non-technical people. Alex reminds them that the clients they're serving are probably a lot better at what they do than the technical person would be.

Alex has been working on networks since he was 11 years old – where he taught himself how networks run while he helped his father's accounting business manage their Novell NetWare system. He helped his high school and many other businesses enter the age of the Internet over the past 25 years.

Prior to Artech, Alex was the youngest Network Engineer at his previous job from the day he started until the day he left. He spent several years in that company and quickly climbed the ranks to become the Senior Network Engineer and the service department manager. In that position he learned a lot about businesses and technology and eventually left to start his own company in 2002.

Alex is driven to solve any problem that comes his way and has a passion for teaching others how to use technology to advance their businesses. With a family background in accounting, he understands the language of business and the numbers that drive it. He can help make your business IT infrastructure into the asset it's meant to be, instead of just another cost center.

Away from the office, Alex enjoys spending time with his wife and children. He often spends weekends working with the animals on their family farm or working on some other project that life on a small farm requires, from updating the electric in the barn to fixing fences. Alex likes sharing his passion for the outdoors with his family as well as his hobbies like camping, hiking and photography.

You can connect with Alex at:
alex@artechsolutions.com
www.linkedin.com/in/alexromp

CHAPTER 3

DATA SECURITY

BY STEPHEN ZETZER

It's a common misconception among business owners that they are not a target for cyber criminals. They believe they are invisible and not worth the efforts of someone who doesn't have good intentions. This isn't true. Being an online target is not about who you are; it's about one simple fact: you are online.

Cyber criminals who look for victims do not care who you are or what your business is. They operate with one mission in mind. That mission is to automatically search for everyone online and see who has open doors. You want your clients to feel welcome, of course, but you definitely don't want the cyber invaders to be a part of that group.

When a cyber criminal finds a locked door, he moves on. However, when he finds an open door, it does not matter whose it is, he will take the next step. The process, or BOT, is programmed to enter through the door into your cyber world. What does it find waiting for it? Credit card information, protected health information, banking information, passwords, and a variety of other nuggets that help the cyber criminals identify just who you are. In many cases, they use what they find to become you through identity theft. Naturally, as a business owner, you don't want that to happen. Numbers are like gold to cyber criminals and they have some very sophisticated software to make the most of what they collect. These are smart people who are operating with bad intentions.

Aside from selling a social security number, something most of us have heard about, have you ever wondered what else goes on with that data that is taken so easily? It is sold to the highest bidder. There's a wide range of activities that take place, ranging from real time auctions and selling bulk credit card numbers to demanding a ransom. If a stolen card number can be validated showing it's legit, the market is going to pay a premium for that.

The purpose of sharing this isn't to frighten business owners. I want businesses to thrive online by taking a stand against cyber attacks and embracing data security. Doing so keeps a business profitable, reputable, and more suited to serve their clients' best interests.

Understanding how people can get into your computer system to compromise it is an important first step. There are many ways in which someone can hack your system. Some widely used methods are:

1) <u>Phishing or spam:</u> Phishing is an email technique that is crafted in a way that it entices someone to open a file or click on a link. For example, you work in accounts payable and you get a 'fake' email message that looks like it comes from your local utility company. It seems legit and it's a business you work with so you open it up because you are compelled to read it. The message actually contains a virus or a link to a site designed to collect your user name and password.

2) <u>Watering hole attack:</u> This is a way of attack using a website that may be used for the general business operation of a particular associate or business partner. For example, if you are a medical office and you routinely visit the website of a health insurance provider and deal with correspondence regarding claim information, billing, etc., you are in a position where you are relying on a business partner to keep their site clean. The criminal organization that has your industry targeted will break into that particular website and place software on it so that when someone is viewing the site, the software will automatically be run. In order for the site to function, standard browser security settings are commonly

lowered or disabled for such a 'trusted site.' The result is through that simple task, part of someone's job, malware is introduced to computers that is designed to look for personal information and report it back to the cybercriminals.

When businesses owners are proactive and understand what they are up against they can reduce the threat of data security breaches. You cannot be 100% safe, but you can do a great deal to learn how to protect your data from attack.

TO ERR IS HUMAN

There was one mid-sized firm, about fifty employees, which I worked with, that really learned the hard way about how crafty and conniving a cyber criminal can be. One of the network users, someone in payroll, received a phishing email that appeared to be from WF Payroll Services. When you are in payroll you don't want any mistakes because people count on those paychecks, and in a small or mid-sized business, they know where to find you to ask what's going on. This was the case with one business.

It was early in the day and the payroll person was planning their work for the day. He went to check his daily spam quarantine report and saw a message that looked legitimate. The person thought that it must have gone there by accident and he opened it up. Well, it wasn't there by accident but the immediate thoughts of this individual didn't process it that way. After all, it seemed familiar and legit. It ended up being a message containing a virus, and by moving it to the inbox, it was now delivered to his computer and was no longer deemed spam. It's important to note that this company did have protection in place and this still happened because a user was convinced to download the message.

The email was opened followed by the attachment. The desktop anti-virus was the last line of defense. It flashed a message: 'Are you certain?' Convinced the message was legit, he replied, 'yes.' The file opened up and within a millisecond, a virus was released onto the entire network.

To fix this significant problem, the office had to be completely shut down for almost twenty-four hours to quarantine and clean up the damage. The ultimate lesson was that you do not want to rely on technology alone to protect you. User education and training is just as important.

EIGHT WAYS TO INCREASE DATA SECURITY

There is no substitute for a user who is educated and cautious about how they are using their computer in the business. It's a balance of technical countermeasures and user awareness that lead to good security. Eight highly effective ways to maximize your business' data security are listed below. Doing all of these well will reduce your risks online.

1) <u>User training:</u> IT is vital to everyone's life, and ignorance and complacency need to be circumvented. There's no more room for "I had no idea." Everyone who interacts with a business has a reasonable expectation that the business owner is protecting their personal and confidential information. The large and ever more frequent data breaches are forcing everyone to raise the bar on what is considered a reasonable level of effort.

2) <u>Have a security gateway device that performs a function called Unified Threat Management (UTM):</u> Imagine everything that comes in and out of your computer is like a constantly moving freight train. UTM is what stands alongside the tracks, stops the train, and opens up every box car and piece of cargo on it to inspect it to ensure that it does not contain something that is not wanted or can cause damage to the network. Purchasing this hardware isn't enough. It must also be properly configured and used. This is best done through a professional monitoring service that provides daily reports. You cannot make assumptions that it is working as expected.

3) <u>Centrally managed anti-malware protection:</u> Malware, the general term, encompasses essentially anything that you

don't want on your network. Most businesses and individuals have anti-virus, but the key for businesses is to have it centrally managed in the cloud. This is important for offices of every size. The downside to depending on the end-user for protection, as opposed to a centrally-managed protection, is that if someone doesn't manually update the protection, it becomes ineffective. Things get overlooked easily this way and you may have different expiration dates for different computers. It's labor intensive, whereas with a centrally managed system anti-malware can be continuously updated and remain intact and effective. It's effective because its part of a consistent process, applied the same way to all computers. This method is truly vital to your success with this defense measure. Many computers and devices don't live in one place anymore. People and their devices are highly mobile, operating from home or on the road. You need a strategy that keeps all devices protected and up to date. If they report to cloud management, they can stay current.

Another consideration to be aware of is that malware can be different and undetectable in a matter of seconds. It is recommended that you check status weekly. The sooner you know something is wrong the better. It's not a question of if, but when malware will hit.

4) Behavior-based protection: Old school anti-malware was signature based, which meant that there was a list of all the known "bad stuff" that the software compared activity against. Today, that list has millions of entries on it and it takes so long for the software to compare the list to the computer that it becomes a drag on performance. Furthermore, it's ineffective because viruses can change signatures so fast that if you are comparing one against ten or twenty million other signatures, the virus may already be new, even within a few seconds. With behavior-based software, the focus is not on the signature. It understands what a piece of software is trying to do and recognizes behavior that is characteristic of

something malicious, based on what it is doing rather than what it is. Behavior-based software adapts on the fly.

5) <u>Data back-up:</u> It's always important to know that you are backing your data up as frequently as possible. See the chapter from my co-author on data backup.

6) <u>Know the software that you are using:</u> There is a tendency for people to rely on free software and it is important that people understand that nothing is truly free. When you are downloading free software, whoever makes it is making a living off that download somehow. Free software is easily subject to manipulation or hijacking and is more likely than ever to contain malware. People tend to click through the license agreements, those long, complicated looking forms in the tiny print. In the licensing agreement it will say that by using the software you are allowing someone to collect information about you. There is ALWAYS some kind of a catch. As a general rule, avoid free software to eliminate the risk.

7) <u>Make use of your particular computer or operating system vendor's application (app) store:</u> Stores such as Apple's or Microsoft's app store, for example, go through a lot of validation and testing to make sure that the content on the store doesn't contain viruses or malware. If you are acquiring apps via downloading them off random websites versus going through the official app store, you are taking a substantial risk.

8) <u>Keep software current:</u> When software is released (e.g., Microsoft Office), it is full of bugs, holes, and risks that no one has thought of yet. They don't get discovered until after the release, when they are sought out, discovered, and then monitored by the software vendors. Cyber criminals are also looking for these "glitches" and when they discover a vulnerability in MS Word, they will expose it. A known bug in the application becomes a conduit to identify you

and your computer. Such bugs can be used to collect your information or inflict damage on someone else. As soon as MS learns about the flaw, they figure it out, correct it, and update it by creating a patch that removes the vulnerability.

You need to have a *bona fide* strategy in place to make sure all computers being used get regular updates. Someone has to centrally monitor and manage all the systems on a network to ensure this happens to every machine on that system.

Within those eight steps is a great deal of information to help businesses take a very active interest in data security for their clients. You can reduce your risks by using these strategies.

DATA SECURITY IS A GROUP EFFORT

All the technology in the world is not going to save a business owner unless the employees also understand the risks of online business and the importance of the data they have access to. Ensure that you have enough education in place about how to recognize when something is starting to go wrong. You need to ensure that all employees get security awareness training. It can be customized to the individual business and it should include training to recognize phishing and spam. Employees should be trained to think or ask before they click on a suspicious link. Having technical protection in place AND educated employees makes for a more prosperous business across the board.

About Stephen

Stephen M. Zetzer, CISSP is the founder and principal owner of eWranglers, LLC. He founded eWranglers in January of 2000 as a Montana firm focused on the Information Security needs of small business. Customers quickly found that secure systems were also reliable systems and the firm has grown to provide quality IT services to clients in Montana and Colorado. The core focus on industry-leading information security practices is still worked in to every client solution.

Stephen's experience includes enterprise level network infrastructure and security consulting through IBM Global Services and other firms. Stephen was a team leader on successful global projects for AT&T, Lucent Technologies, TCI (now Comcast), and JD Edwards (now Oracle), among others. Stephen also has experience providing information security training to private sector, military and healthcare clients.

A graduate of the Indiana University Kelly School of Business, Stephen holds the Certified Information Systems Security Professional (CISSP) credential. The CISSP is considered by many in the industry to be the highest level certification available. In the 1990s, Stephen was among the first Microsoft Certified Systems Engineers, of which there are tens of thousands today.

Today, eWranglers focuses on providing a balance of: performance, functionality, risk, and cost to its clients with respect to their information technology. The entire company is designed from the ground up to deliver predictable results at predictable costs to clients who seek out its services. They believe in what they do and sell – to the extent that they operate their own fully digital office with end-to-end automation. Their Bozeman, MT office runs on a hybrid cloud-based and locally-hosted architecture. With Stephen's guidance, eWranglers is dedicated to constantly learning and always improving what they do.

CHAPTER 4

SECURITY IN THE AGE OF SOCIAL MEDIA

BY DAVID SZYMANSKI

THE WAY WE COMMUNICATE IN THE 2010'S

Social media is an inescapable and rapidly expanding fact of life in the second decade of the 21st Century, with over a billion and a half people engaged in some form of it. LinkedIn, Facebook and Twitter are the most popular sites but there are hundreds of others at least, from Instagram and YouTube to gaming forums. People are using their smartphones more for social media than as a phone these days. According to a recent article in the *New York Times*, a spokesperson for Vonage said that voicemails left on phones are down 8 percent in the past six months alone. A 2012 report found that teens are texting more and making phone calls less. I was watching *Good Morning America* not long ago, and news anchor Amy Robach admitted that she never even checks her voicemail. Everyone knows if they want to get a hold of her, they should probably text. Between texting and all of the social media sites, we're definitely communicating in a lot of new ways we could not have fathomed even 15 years ago.

BOTS AND BAD, SHORT URLS

But as with every wonderful technology, the proliferation of social media has inherent risks to personal security – that are certainly not much fun to think about when we're talking to our friends via a variety of portals and gadgets. At some point when PCs and Macs became part of our lives, we realized the need for anti-virus software to counter the power of data and system-destroying viruses and malware. And despite all of the security measures we think we have taken, cybercrime is still on the rise. Cybercriminals are creating their own "bots" – codes that go out and search for data via openings in computer security systems.

The criminals aren't even sitting at their machines – they're letting their bots go out there and do the hacking for them! It used to be that big companies were the ones fighting this problem with people trying to break into the data of Fortune 500 companies, but bots are programmed to look for millions of sites and try to find one that hasn't been patched with proper security. They don't discriminate between small dental practices and major corporations; finding a way in through an unsecured passage is their aim, and they can cause a lot of damage. People do it for a variety of reasons. Some will send ransom notes demanding money for your data. Russian and Chinese cyber-criminals are known to look for credit card numbers. Others try to find banking passwords to transfer money out of un-secure accounts. Some just do it to prove they can, test their brilliance and gain their 15 minutes of fame.

One of the ways these high tech criminals are breaking into our lives is through bad URLS, which are the website addresses you type in. If someone misspells "Bank of America" when they do online banking, more than likely they'll end up on a "phishing" site, which may look like the real B of A but isn't. And when you type your user name and password into that site, you're giving important information to the bad guys. On social media sites like Facebook, many links use short URLs that use the designation similar to "bit.ly" with some type of six digit character for the website address. These are a bit more insidious. If you receive a text or tweet with a long URL you can see that it's misspelled, but if you receive one of these short URLs, you can't tell if it's legit or not. Short URLs are ubiquitous on Facebook, LinkedIn and Twitter, and it's important that you trust where the link came from and what website it is taking you to. You won't know you're on the wrong site until you go there.

OTHER CONCERNS AND PRIVACY ISSUES

It goes without saying that we should be careful accepting friend or LinkedIn requests from total strangers – yet in the social media environment we do this all the time, thinking nothing bad can come of it. As often as not, they're not there to be your friend and make a contact but to have access to your life and information. Some people hijack people's pages and steal the identity of your real friends, then send a friend request. When you get a new friend request from someone who is a longtime friend, check it out to make sure the new request is legit – because it may be fake.

There are tons of phishing scams out there and the "phishermen" are increasingly inventive. As I mentioned, sometimes you'll have an innocent enough looking link to a page that looks like a Facebook or PayPal home page and prompts you to log in, but instead it is only collecting your username and password. Sometimes it's not just about stealing financial information. There are those who find ways to impersonate people or companies on FB and submit inappropriate posts and misinformation in their name. My wife and business partner Cathy once found herself in an IM conversation with a "friend" on FB and they said something out of character. Cathy called the "friend" on the telephone, and she was not on FB and someone else was posing as her. This is a new method of identity theft to be aware of.

So how do you combat this? On each of the social media sites, you can configure what people can see. There's no right or wrong answer on how to prevent such breaches – you just have to be aware of what you're posting and why and who can see it. Do you think, for instance, that your personal cell number should be on your LinkedIn page? And what about your home address? These are dangerous things to have online, because clever cybercriminals can use that basic contact information to seek out more data related to your life. When you sign up for these sites, you should be careful how you configure things and be aware of the ramifications of what you allow.

GPS DATA

Whether they use their social media outlets for business or personal use, parents should also be very careful about putting the names of their children anywhere strangers can see it. They should also know that when most phones take pictures, they store the GPS data of when and where it was taken. So if you post a pic of your child's soccer practice, it's possible for people to know where and when they play soccer. Fortunately, you can remove the location data from photos with the flick of a tab – but if you don't do this beforehand, make sure before you post the pic that the location data is individually removed. A stalker could easily use this to lure your child at a later time. And as we know, stalkers aren't just after children.

Many social media sites have location based tracking, and if this is activated or not turned off, it can be used to keep track of where you are at any time. In general having GPS data on photos taken on your cell is a fantastic idea. Twenty years from now, you'll be able to identify where and when any pic was taken. Just be careful how you advertise that. People check in every place they go because they think it's cool. Just make sure only the people you want to know that can see it.

SURVEY SAID...

Finally, be careful of those fun and simple surveys. I see these posted on Facebook all the time. Which movie are you? Which President? Which character on "Monty Python" or "Mad Men"? Some of the questions are innocuous enough but others in the mix may be similar to typical security questions you are asked on secure sites like your email or bank accounts. So now that you've answered that your favorite color is blue and you went to this specific grade school and your first dog's name was Sam, if the survey was created by a cybercriminal, they now have your email address and can put all the information together to cause a lot of trouble. Sure, most of these surveys are legit, but you need to be careful.

POLICIES

In dealing with companies in an IT capacity, one of the most important things we need to determine is, what are your goals as far as social media goes? Do you want to expand your brand or improve customer service by having an outlet where people can ask questions? Have Frequently Asked Questions (FAQ) or a Forum? Figure those things out first and then determine who needs access to it. If you're running a company, you may not want every employee to have the ability to post something on your social media pages. Think of the bad publicity celebrities get from kneejerk Twitter posts that they later have to apologize for. People often post without thinking first. So you need to limit access.

Also, these days, most of us have a lot of online accounts with different user names and passwords – but some of us fail to keep good records of these accounts. Say you open an Instagram account but then forget you have it. And in the meantime while you're neglecting it, someone has hacked into it and is using it to impersonate you. It's important to keep track of these things you are signed up for, whether it's a business or personal account.

And if you're a business, you need to enforce whatever policies are in place. If only certain employees are allowed to post on your FB page, you need to make sure everyone knows that and review and update these policies frequently as social media evolves. If you created your social media policy three years ago, well, doesn't that leave out things like Snapchat that didn't exist in 2011? Every few months there is a new site, so policies should be updated and new concerns should be addressed.

Another big phenomenon taking place in companies today is BYOD, or Bring Your Own Device. A lot of companies are letting employees bring in their own phones or tablets that allow them to work with sensitive data outside the office computer network. Are your employees allowed to post to the company's social media sites from their personal devices? And what happens if an employee leaves the company? Does the company have any control over that person's ability to post something on Facebook? The policies you create upfront with your employees need to specify how things are handled with BYOD.

One more issue should go without saying but people often take them for granted: having strong passwords. You should change them often. Most social media sites don't force you to change them so you can have the same one year after year. But let's say someone steals it. They might not use it today, they may just be out there creating a collection of accounts for when they want to start messing with you. So it's best to change your passwords frequently before they can access it. And be careful not to use the same passwords on multiple sites. There are millions of LinkedIn passwords stolen and posted online. So if you use the same one for LinkedIn as you use for Facebook, the thieves would also have your FB password – and maybe the one for your banking!

MONITORING AND OTHER SAFEGUARDS

You need to keep track of all these accounts you set up and actively monitor them, so that you can detect if there is a problem or if anyone is posting things about your company that shouldn't be there. Besides the aforementioned password changes, make sure no one has unauthorized access to those passwords, and use all the technology at your disposal to help prevent you from getting hacked or clicking on the wrong thing. Be as thorough as possible setting up firewalls, anti-virus software and anti-malware software – and make sure your mobile hotspots are properly encrypted. If you go to a diner for breakfast and suddenly get a Wi-Fi connection, make sure it's a legitimate one. Anyone can take a Verizon hub in and call it by the name of the establishment and log everything all the patrons are typing.

Also, use a VPN to connect back to your company's network. Encrypt all traffic so that even if someone is snooping on a wireless system, it will be encrypted so that it won't make any sense to them. Keep in mind, none of those things will do you any good if your virus definitions are over a week old, so update your firewall and virus definitions frequently. I'd also like to recommend a growing Social Media Management dashboard that allows you to manage multiple social networks, schedule tweets and messages and track brand mentions, analyze social media traffic. One of its best uses is as a content planner for LinkedIn, Facebook and Twitter; you can go in and create posts that you want to schedule for these sites. That way all your content can be thought out and properly edited rather than posted on the fly as some people and companies do, which allows for content errors.

SOME PARTING TIPS

I recommend that you use URLs with https (note the s) whenever possible, which encrypts the connection so that that passwords and content you type in is protected. It's also advisable to use locks on your mobile devices whenever possible. This is a general security issue because if you post Twitter and FB content from your phone and you accidentally leave it somewhere, anyone who picks it up can impersonate you. And if you use these devices for posting business content, make sure they have software that allows you to remotely wipe the device if it's stolen. If you're an employee engaging in BYOD, make sure that you are as protected using your phone or pad at home as you are with the firewall you have at work. If you're sitting at a bar or coffee shop, what protection do you have there when you're on those social sites?

Finally, there's etiquette. Be respectful of other's comments. Remember you are not obligated to comment on every post you read. And think carefully about your response before sending. Remember it's your reputation and security that can be affected if you don't take the proper precautions.

About David

As a recognized technology leader, David Szymanski is president of Szymanski Consulting, which he founded in 1978. David's experience ranges from working with The Department of Energy to working with Long Care Nursing Facilities, Schools, Non-Profit Organizations and Small Businesses.

Szymanski Consulting is a long-standing member of the Manufacturer's Association, Chamber of Commerce, Erie Network Users Group and Technology Council of Northwest Pennsylvania. Their specialty is Network Services, IT consulting and Computer Support serving businesses in Erie, Meadville and Fairview, Pennsylvania.

"Our philosophy is simple, we treat others as we would like to be treated. This philosophy has allowed our company to grow and prosper with long-term customers," remarked David. "We are not looking for quick sales, we are building long-term relationships." David considers each client's bottom line, budget and expectations while strengthening their infrastructure to boost their productivity and profitability.

In David's spare time, he enjoys spending time with his lovely wife of twenty years, Cathy. David is on the board for the North Western Pennsylvania Technology Committee, he also serves on the board for The Kiwanis Club of Erie, Pennsylvania. He is the secretary for the Pennsylvania State Police Camp Cadet program as well as the president of the Erie Network Users Group. David can be found volunteering wherever there is a need in the community. David and Cathy have two Dachshunds and one Maine Coon cat – Wilbur, Oscar and Roxie – and enjoy traveling, gardening, reading and biking.

CHAPTER 5

MANAGED SERVICES: IS IT RIGHT FOR YOUR BUSINESS?

BY JEFF WILDER

In recent years "Managed Services" has become somewhat of a buzzword in the Information Technology (IT) Support world. This concept has also led to the formation of hundreds of IT companies around the world functioning as a Managed Service Provider or MSP. While the MSP strategy began as a service to large companies, it has evolved to the point that now any size business can take advantage of these services in a very cost effective way.

Today, the general role of the MSP for business is to take on a broad position within a company's IT structure, enabling the business to run more efficiently, stay up to date on the latest technology, and avoid any significant downtime that could potentially rob the business of considerable revenue. As a simple definition, a qualified MSP will function as your full corporate IT team "in a box" and you should be able to depend upon them as your complete IT solution for all your current and future business needs.

As the owner of an IT business since the mid 1990's, I have had the opportunity to evolve with this concept and develop my business into a state-of-the-art Managed Service Provider. In fact, my company was doing "Managed Services" before it was even known as "Managed Services." Initially, we would go out and perform all the "plumbing" work that needed to be done to establish a business' network, run maintenance, run cleanups, do system optimizations, backup check reviews and things of that nature. As we slowly started to build clientele we also consistently expanded our services portfolio and have continuously grown to become a highly respected MSP.

As small businesses continue to develop their dependency on technology to operate efficiently and compete effectively in their market space, they find the IT resources needed are constantly becoming more complex. For most businesses, the days of "Break-Fix" IT management have become a thing of the past. The "Break-Fix" concept simply meant if something IT related broke you would call your IT professional to fix it and sometimes the fixes took days. Whereas, in an MSP environment, the entire goal is to prevent things from breaking down so you can minimize your business downtime and maximize your productivity. If you don't stay on top of things such as backups, patches and security, it will not be a matter of "if" you will face an IT outage; it will simply be a matter of "when" you will face an outage and to what extent your business will suffer as a result.

My approach to managed services may be somewhat different than that of others in that I don't believe managed services is for every organization. However, there are particular organizations for which managed services makes a lot of sense. Generally speaking they are organizations that value IT as well as the tools and technology that enable them to do their business more efficiently and more cost effectively. A quality MSP can enable a company to gain more productivity and more visibility so they can make better decisions. Of course, not everyone falls into that category, so I don't see an MSP as a one-size-fits-all solution for every entity.

WHY THE MANAGED SERVICE PROVIDER CONCEPT WORKS

The primary benefit to incorporating an MSP into your business strategy is that it then becomes a team effort and a collaboration. In a Break-Fix world, when the business was down, the IT company made money and when the business was running smoothly the IT company lost money. The MSP concept fixes that dichotomy and allows both the business and the IT company to partner in keeping the company up and running with little to no noticeable down time.

To accommodate our business customers, we have every level of engineer and technician so that no matter what type of problem the business has with their technology, we can offer the support necessary no matter the size of the issue, not only from a knowledge and experience level, but also from a team perspective.

A true MSP is a self-performer when it comes to taking responsibility for your IT needs. I like to say they are "pot committed." If you ever played "Texas Hold'em" you will know that term to mean "you're all in." For a service provider, that means they have invested in their own infrastructure and built out their own services rather than outsourcing services to another IT company. To put it another way, you want a provider that has full "skin in the game" regarding how they are managing and supporting you.

Our approach to Managed Services is that we don't outsource any service we provide. We 'self-perform' everything—our oncall services, data center, managed service platform, helpdesk, field engineers, consultants, etc.; every person is a W-2 wage employee. From a stability standpoint as well as from a quality control perspective, it's extremely important that the provider self-perform their work and it eliminates the finger pointing when there is an issue.

We do not outsource key and critical roles to others and rely on them to deliver it. If there is a problem with the delivery of any aspect of my client's IT needs, we are fully responsible and cannot blame any failures on someone to whom we outsourced one of the services. That's when you know your service provider has "skin in the game."

THREE GENERAL COMPONENTS OF MANAGED SERVICES

There are three general categories of service you can expect from your MSP, which include Infrastructure, Strategy and Support. Let's look at each of these in more detail.

I. Infrastructure

Managing your IT infrastructure is the "plumbing" side of the business. This includes the actual installation of the routers, switches, hardware, etc. and making sure everything is secure, reliable and stable. It also involves staying up-to-date on all necessary maintenance, monitoring 24/7/365 and doing verifications against the monitoring activity. In my office, we do automate a lot of things within our managed service practice, but we also audit the automation with an actual physical check from our maintenance engineers on a regular basis. It is very important that your MSP is physically monitoring all the automation to make sure everything is running as it should. Unfortunately, I have seen too many cases where businesses thought things were running properly only to find out part of the automation had failed and no one knew.

The specific areas of attention given by your MSP inside your IT Infrastructure should include the following:

- System Maintenance
- Patch Management
- System Optimization
- Security
- Disaster Recovery and Business Continuity
- Network Administrator

II. Strategy

As an MSP we work alongside our clients in technology consulting and project planning, becoming their virtual Chief Information Officer or vCIO. We help our clients from a strategic perspective with their IT in that we aid them in getting their IT in alignment with their corporate objectives. The main question here is, "Where are they as a company headed over the next 3 to 5 years and how does their current IT stack up?" Based on their response to that question, we are able to give them the type of counseling and support that will help them achieve their objectives. As part of our ongoing strategy consulting, we also conduct face-to-face technology reviews on a quarterly basis so we can do any necessary realigning.

Another important component related to strategy is conducting a Business Impact Analysis – when the company is looking at incorporating new technology or possibly different software. Through this analysis we are able to evaluate how that will impact the environment from a user, productivity and budget perspective.

A third key component of strategy is to assist with the company's annual technology planning and obsolescence scheduling. Through a coordinated effort with the appropriate company personnel, we guide them through determining what is working efficiently, what enhancements they should be considering, and what systems or software have become obsolete and need to be retired.

Your Managed Service Provider should also be well equipped to help you with compliance issues. HIPAA, for example, is a very pressing compliance concern for many, especially those in the healthcare industry. Your MSP should not only ensure you are in compliance from an IT perspective, but they should also help you build the compliance policy by which you are guided. Unfortunately, when it comes to compliance issues, there are many in the IT industry who don't even realize that IT providers are required to be HIPAA compliant themselves. As a result they are not performing risk assessments, they don't have their policy manuals built, they don't have their protocols and procedures in place and they are playing with fire. There are severe penalties for HIPAA non-compliance (as well as with other non-compliance issues). So, if you are a healthcare related business, make sure to ask your potential MSP to show you their HIPAA compliance policy book. If they don't have one, that's a company you should cross off your list.

To summarize, the following points should be part of the Strategy assistance you receive from your MSP:

They should function as your Virtual Chief Information Office or vCIO and assist you in:

1. Quarterly Technology Business Review Meetings

2. System Design Resources

3. Technology Business Impact Planning

4. Annual Budgeting

5. Asset Management

6. Equipment Procurement and Delivery

7. Compliance Support

III. Support

Providing comprehensive support for your company's IT System involves having an appropriately staffed helpdesk and knowledgeable and responsive field staff. This means being available to respond to your specific IT needs 24/7/365. This includes the administrative function of day in and day out management of your system, adding and deleting users, and things of that nature.

Specific items under this category will include such things as:

- Helpdesk Support
- Onsite and In-shop Services
- Project management

IS AN MSP COST EFFECTIVE AND HOW DOES IT COMPARE TO HAVING IN-HOUSE IT PERSONNEL?

There are definite business cases for how much more budget-friendly managed services can be versus hiring staff internally. Hiring an MSP makes more sense in many cases because it is usually less costly than to employee your own in-house IT staff. Of course, each business must perform their own due diligence to make that determination. If you employ one person to handle your in-house IT needs or what we refer to as a "single person environment, you must ask yourself some important questions.

1.) What happens when that one person is on vacation? Or when they have to call in sick? Or who is manning the system on holidays when they are with their family? With an MSP all your IT needs are covered 24/7/365.

2.) Does that one person know everything they need to know to keep the business running as effectively and efficiently as possible? Remember, your IT is limited by that one person's knowledge. More times than not, businesses are not going to spend the money on a true network administrator or senior level engineer. They usually will hire a technician at thirty to forty thousand dollars and expect them to completely manage their infrastructure. Well, that's completely impractical. That would be like hiring a recent college graduate with an accounting degree and making them your controller or CFO. Frankly, you're just trying to get something cheap, but expecting more from that person. In fact, you will be only setting that person up for failure and likely will be setting your business up for failure as well.

3.) Can one person effectively handle all of our IT needs? Think of this comparison. If you have a project, for example, to replace 20 PC's, how long will it take for your in-house IT person to do that keeping in mind that it will then pull them away from their other responsibilities. The answer is, "A long time!" while their other responsibilities have to be put on hold. Whereas in an MSP environment, when we assign a few field techs to install 20 PC's for a customer, that doesn't impact our helpdesk, the network management team or any of the other services we are providing. So, the other users don't feel the impact of reduced services.

4.) What is the real cost of hiring an in-house IT person? As a business owner you know there is a significant cost burden when hiring any employee. In addition to their salary, you have expenses related to insurance, vacations, taxes, unemployment expenses, etc. When you outsource that service, you don't have to worry about those additional expenses.

5.) What hoops will you have to jump through to terminate an employee if they are not doing their job to meet your standards? No doubt there will be coaching, a verbal warning, a written warning, then a final written warning depending on the laws of your state and your corporate

HR policy. The point is that it's not always an easy task to terminate an employee. Then you have to worry about hiring a replacement. Whereas, if you have a contracted MSP, you can fire your MSP at any time and move on if you don't feel like the relationship is working out. Since your MSP is a contractor it places the pressure on them to perform or you can simply discharge them and bring in another firm. It takes things to a whole new level of accountability. We, as an MSP, have to be right 100% of the time.

As an MSP, we have to perform above and beyond the business' expectations. We don't have the luxury of telling the user that just called in, "Wait until tomorrow, I should have time then." We have to take care of that issue right now. There is always a sense of urgency with an MSP, whereas, I have observed that a number of internal IT personnel have a tendency to become complacent. In many cases, it's simply a job or paycheck to them. They aren't driven or motivated to grow and improve. My intention is not to be disparaging toward internal IT hires, and I realize not all internal IT people can be described in that way, but unfortunately I see that more often than not.

6.) Finally, where is an internal IT person going to grow to if he's a lone wolf in a company? There is no career development plan for him to grow toward, and usually the good IT people will leave a dead-end job as they find other opportunities available to them.

IS AN MSP RIGHT FOR MY BUSINESS?

The answer is "yes" if you are interested in increased operational efficiency, reduced operating costs, minimized downtime, being able to run your business instead of your technology, and having peace of mind knowing your network is monitored 24/7/365. A qualified MSP can assist you in achieving those goals.

About Jeff

An expert in the technologies required by small and medium-sized businesses, Jeff Wilder acts as Virtual Chief Information Officer for many clients. For nearly two decades, Jeff Wilder has led Atlanta-based Century Solutions Group to grow from four employees to thirty-three. As President, he directs his consulting and engineering staff to serve Century Solutions Group's 200+ clients.

Jeff Wilder finds variety and purpose in his work. He said, "I love the challenge that every day is different, and we have to continue learning and growing to stay ahead. I love solving problems and providing technology solutions that allow our clients to succeed."

Serving the Southeastern U.S., including Georgia, North Carolina, South Carolina, Alabama, Florida and Tennessee, Century started out as just a hardware reseller and slowly morphed into a comprehensive Managed Service Provider. Today's Century provides consulting, systems integration, telephony, software development, cloud services and strategic planning, in addition to extensive managed service solutions branded as Intelligent Networks.

Besides countless hours of 'on the job' consulting and engineering for his clients, Jeff earned a B.B.A., Computer Information Systems, from Georgia State University. He holds the following certifications: A+, MSCE, MCITP, CCEA, VCP, CCA and CCS. Jeff insists that his engineers also get certifications, keeping company standards high.

Jeff Wilder's clients appreciate that he's straightforward. He tells them, "We are accountable and responsive. We do make mistakes, but will always own up and correct them to the best of our abilities."

Information technology continues to evolve, so it's Jeff's priority to continually adapt. Besides keeping his mind moving on to what's ahead for business technology, Jeff makes sure he's physically ready. Crossfit, running half and full marathons and golf are his sports choices, as well as fishing and hunting.

With two small children, Mason and Molly Claire, Disney World is the favorite family destination for Jeff and his wife, Alli. Jeff plays Legos and games with his children, and enjoys movies and spending time with his family.

CHAPTER 6

DISASTER RECOVERY

BY AMANDA HARPER

Businesses use information technology (IT) to process data quickly and effectively. It's how we work, it's what we do. We use email and share data across a multitude of locations and devices. The scope of the technology we rely on to manage and communicate data internally and externally is extensive. Data is crucial and important. In fact, it's the most important commodity a business owns and that business's survival and continued operation is completely reliant on that data.

But what happens when your IT resources stop working for you or aren't accessible? Without a plan in place, even basic business operations become near impossible, staff stress increases dramatically, and the business goes into reactive mode, resulting in even greater risk as decisions are made hastily and without a proper understanding of the impact those decisions have on the present moment AND the future. Why not put a plan in place ahead of time that covers a range of eventualities and helps guide staff – so that the right choices are made and the business operates as efficiently as possible even when the worst of disasters strikes?

The general definition of Disaster Recovery is: the process of returning a business to its normal processes and operation after a disruptive event, whether a natural disaster or an electronic disaster, a large or small disruption. Creating a Disaster Recovery Plan (DRP) to deal with these unwelcomed, unexpected situations allows for a resource of well-thought out processes, policies, and procedures that assist you in recovering or continuing IT services after the disaster. It's a plan that works for your specific business and is focused on returning your business to standard operating procedure as quickly as possible.

ANTICIPATE A DISASTER

No one can predict when a disruption to business will occur or exactly what form that disruption will be so it is important to build the plan ahead of time. This can be a challenge, as you need to evaluate your operations and the various scenarios of what can go wrong. With that evaluation you can build a 'What If' type of plan. Of course, this is not an easy process and can take resources away from your business to get it done. Our recommendation is that you should create your DRP with an IT professional who is familiar with your business and how you use your technology resources. They can help you put all the pieces together, assess key components, and define how you will mitigate the risks and return to normal operations.

One morning, we received an alert that a critical server at a client site was offline. The other servers in the office were operating correctly so we knew right away that it wasn't a simple power or Internet outage. We quickly determined what was wrong and consulted the client's Disaster Recovery Plan, which indicated that this system had to be returned to operation as quickly as possible. This server had just gone out of warranty and was planned for replacement but the downturn in the economy had delayed that process. The part we needed would normally have been available within four hours; however, with the server being out of warranty, it would be two days before it was available. With this knowledge we went back to the DRP, briefed the client about what we could do, and decided to use their backup system to virtualize the server. With the backup appliance taking a snapshot of the client's servers every hour there was minimal data loss and the virtualized server meant that the team could return to normal operations quickly and with minimal disruption. This worked because of the plan and having a backup solution that backed up the entire system.

Two lessons were learned from this. First, the plan gave direction and assurance for a more effective resolution. Second, the client fully understood how risky it is to have equipment without a warranty and never delayed equipment replacement or warranty extension again.

Another client of ours was in the middle of a major project—relocating their office to a new city. They knew there were some risks inherent in the move but had measures in place, including a well-thought out DRP. Once onsite at the new office, we started up the client's systems and they didn't work. During the move there had been a massive failure in their data storage system affecting multiple servers. As part of their DRP, we had a backup system that took server images hourly and allowed us to virtualize those images in the event of a disaster. Coupled with a backup of those images at a remote datacenter, we were confident that this bump in the road could be overcome. We briefed the client that a complicated piece of hardware had failed during the move and that we were going to invoke their DRP. Everyone understood what that meant and their systems were up and fully operational (on the backup appliance) before the planned start of business following the physical move.

This experience shows how having a proper discussion between a client and IT professionals helps to ensure that a client's needs are understood. Simplify, understand, and rationalize. According to an HP and SCORE survey: a company that experiences a computer outage that lasts more than ten days will never fully recover financially and 50% will be out of business within five years. Major data losses usually result in being out of business within one year. Not having a good DRP may mean the end of your business.

THE FOUR DISASTERS

A DRP is a means for business continuity in the event of a disaster that impacts part or all of a business's resources. The plan has to have a goal and an understanding of what its purpose is. For most, the goal is to resume normal operating capabilities as quickly as possible while minimizing downtime and data loss.

Most small and mid-size businesses do not have a plan in place. Then they have a disruption that impacts their business. Mid-crisis is not the time to establish a plan. It's not a matter of if an event will occur; it's a matter of when. You may experience:

1) Natural disasters: Tornado, earthquake, flooding, severe thunderstorms, or other weather-related disasters.

2) Hardware failure: In my experience, this failure is the number one cause of downtime for small and medium-sized businesses. Servers go down, workstations crash, business applications fail, critical printers may stop working, and other equipment related disruptions may impact a business.

3) Software failure: Not having software patches routinely updated or assessing how those patches may impact a workstation or network can cause downtime. Operating systems can stop being supported and no longer get upgrades. Then they fail, leaving you with no means of ever retrieving the lost data. Also, viruses and malware can have a huge impact on businesses if precautions such as business-grade firewalls and email scanning aren't used. According to Symantec, an Internet security company, in 2013 over 30% of all attacks were targeted at small businesses. In 2011, that number was 18%. Hackers and cyber thieves are interested in small businesses.

4) Human error: Technology fails but humans also err. It can be intentional or accidental. A user on a server may accidentally delete files or entire mailboxes, or data could be deleted as a deliberate act of sabotage.

Regardless of the type of disaster, business owners can do something to protect their data and their business and that is to develop a Disaster Recovery Plan. Then the plan needs to be tested and updated as the business grows and changes. A DRP is only as good as the last test of the plan.

ELEVEN SMART MOVES FOR DISASTER RECOVERY

We cannot predict disaster, but we can predict their possible effects allowing us to plan in advance. There are many facets of business and at times, it's hard to take them all into account. When developing a plan, it should be done in conjunction with an IT professional.Here are some ideas that you should factor into your plan, as they will make all the difference.

1) Understand your business and how it works. Create an outline or blueprint of all the hardware, software, and data systems that are used by the business in network and know how all the hardware/software apps work together. This makes it easier to restore a network. It's also great for insurance claims for physical spaces that experience losses.

2) Identify areas of vulnerability. Evaluate everything from operating procedures to the current plans for protecting data. Look at contingency planning. If something goes wrong, what are you going to do?

3) Recovery Time and Recovery Point Objectives. Known as RTO and RPO, these will indicate the maximum amount of time in which business processes or functions must be restored after a disaster or interruption. How long can a business be down before being impacted? How old can the data be?

4) Develop both short-term and long-term plans. Once you develop an RTO and RPO, you need to identify which operations within a business are most critical to be up and running first. For example, a call center would likely make it a priority to have telephones up and running first because they are critical to operations. The short-term plan will layout the procedures to do that and dedicate resources toward it. Once critical activities and operations are up and running, what is the longer RTO? What can take a back seat? Scanning to email, for example, may be secondary. This is the second stage of recovery. By the end, everything is up and running.

5) <u>Keep the plans in multiple places.</u> The following people or places should have a copy: Your IT professional, key business executives should keep a copy offsite, and you should have a copy onsite in a fireproof safe.

6) <u>Establish an alternate operating location.</u> We live in a world where many jobs allow one to work from anywhere. If something were to happen to your physical office where would you work? Find out and test it periodically. At least once a quarter staff should work remotely to see if the mobility function is working to protect against interruption from physical space. Also, ensure that IT can access and maintain systems remotely. In addition, have alternate numbers and email addresses for getting a hold of staff.

7) <u>Get a secondary Internet service.</u> If your business relies on the Internet, you should get a secondary Internet service provider. Any business with cloud-based applications can benefit from this security measure because you have less tolerance of Internet downtime.

8) <u>Work with IT for the best data back-up solutions.</u> There are many factors to consider: what data needs to be backed up, how should it be backed up, and how often should those backups occur. Manual backup systems where tapes (real old school) or backup drives are manually swapped and rotated offsite are better than nothing, but the best solution is to automate backups to eliminate human error. For faster recovery times, a backup that takes an image of an entire system is best and allows that system to be virtualized on a backup appliance in the event of a disaster. This means the system will operate just like the users are familiar with and will make recovery much easier. Even better is that these types of systems are designed to backup locally, and to the cloud, as frequently as every hour; this reduces data loss risk, reduces recovery time, and it eliminates someone forgetting to take the backup home. In one solution, you significantly reduce the risk of human error while meeting and possibly

exceeding all the recovery objectives for your company.

9) <u>Have an off-site back-up site.</u> Even when you have data back-up onsite you want to have it in the cloud, as well.

10) <u>Maintain systems.</u> Keep equipment up to date to help avoid hardware/software failures.

11) <u>Testing.</u> This can't be mentioned enough! You won't know if your plan works unless you test.

GET IT DONE

Disasters are always unwelcomed but they don't have to be devastating to your business. Smart business owners take steps to protect what they've worked so hard to build. Having a *Disaster Recovery Plan* makes sense and it could possibly make or break your business's ability to rebound from a disaster.

About Amanda

Amanda Harper is president of Gaeltek, LLC I Technology Solutions in Manassas, Virginia. She oversees day-to-day management of non-technical operations. She co-founded Gaeltek in 2004 and joined the company full-time in 2009.

Previously, Ms. Harper was a spokesperson and press officer in the Office of Press Relations at the United States Department of State from July 2005 through July 2009. She was responsible for explaining U.S. policy on international issues to U.S. and foreign media audiences. She also represented the U.S. Department of State in interagency meetings, planning sessions, and international exercises to test and strengthen the United States government's response to cyber-attacks and other incidents of national significance. Before joining the Office of Press Relations, she served as Public Affairs Specialist in the Bureau of Population, Refugees and Migration (April 2004 – July 2005) where she designed and implemented press and public outreach strategies to enhance the public's understanding of the United States Refugee Program.

From May 2002 to April 2004, Ms. Harper was the Information Officer for the Bureau of East Asian and Pacific Affairs, where she managed the public affairs outreach program, responded to media inquiries and maintained routine contact with foreign and domestic journalists on diverse issues affecting the Asia-Pacific region. From June 2000 to May 2002, Ms. Harper was a program analyst with the U. S. Department of the Navy. She served as the Deputy Director, Small and Disadvantaged Business Utilization, where she counseled and assisted small and disadvantaged businesses with procurement regulations and practices, determined the appropriate buying office for their product, and provided pertinent data on Department of Defense procurements. She was also the Assistant Lead for Earned Value Management Systems and evaluated contract status by analyzing contractors' use of internal cost and schedule management control systems to ensure that actual work performed met technical cost and schedule requirements, resource planning, and operational schedules. Ms. Harper joined the United States government as a Presidential Management Fellow.

Ms. Harper is the co-author of *Business IT 101: A Business Owner's Guide for Finding Hassle-Free Computer Support* (2011). She holds a B.A. in Political Science from Bridgewater College; her M.P.A. in Public Administration is from Virginia Commonwealth University.

Ms. Harper is the recipient of numerous United States Government awards and honors, including from the U. S. Department of State, the U.S. Department of the Navy, and from the U. S. Department of Homeland Security for her commitment and efforts to testing and strengthening the government's response to cyber-attacks.

CHAPTER 7

APPS IN THE CLOUD: 10 THINGS YOU NEED TO CONSIDER

BY ROBERT BOLES

1. WHERE ARE THE CLOUDS?

I have written in the past about multi-site network solutions and the difference between private and public wide area networks and connections. With all these applications now based in the "clouds," what's happening is that consumers are now emulating what has been a traditional business model in that all of these apps are being delivered from a resource that is "away" from them, in the cloud.

When you say "cloud," the term itself is ambiguous to some degree. Fifteen years ago, when engineers would get together and talk network design, the space in between sites connected via networks was always depicted as a "cloud." Where and what the cloud is – is always a matter of perspective. If you are located where I am based, say, in Northern California, and you go out of the area to receive something on the Internet, you could say anything hosted anywhere beyond your home could hypothetically be in the cloud, because it's not on your hard drive. The term "cloud" is ambiguous because there is not a clear definition of where something resides. Today the term "cloud" in general means that the data and computing power is on the Internet somewhere.

2. THE DIFFERENCE IN SPEED

The purpose of this chapter is to understand why you need to do certain things in order to have a positive experience getting to the cloud. What that means is making sure the environment of the local network is well put together, because the better your network and ISP connectivity is, the better you and your teams experience will be. It's all correlated. Everything comes down to the fact that all these apps and services we deal with on a personal and business level, including voicemails, emails, videos and file sharing, are located in the cloud now, and no longer stored locally on a LAN (Local Area Network) based server which runs on much faster access bandwidth than the cloud service.

Traditionally, applications would live on a server on a LAN where all the machines would access via connection throughput of 10, 100, and today 1000 megabits per second (mbps). But when apps are in the cloud, the access speeds are much slower, like 1.5 mbps (as on DSL) or 20+mbps download cable. In the past, these apps were accessed locally over higher speeds, and users have been used to things working quickly. But when you go now to the cloud, those same apps are accessed over a single connection to the Internet with less bandwidth than a LAN. Thus, the Internet connections are slow in comparison to those on the LAN.

It's pretty simple mathematically. If a LAN is traveling at 1000 megabits per second, and the Internet connection is downloading at 20 mgs, that's a huge difference. We're used to pulling all these apps at ridiculously high speeds but this slows them up. People sometimes ignore this because they believe that they can just have any quality network and still have a positive experience with the apps. I'm essentially saying that with apps existing in the clouds now, the quality of your network and Internet connection is more critical than ever. So it's best to have a solid plan in place to solidify your connectivity to the cloud so you can have the best experience and most productivity in using those apps.

3. WHAT DO YOU WANT TO ACCOMPLISH?

When we are setting up a client's system, we first need to understand what you are trying to accomplish. The ideal circumstance is when we are engaged by clients up front and guide the network design process, helping our clients avoid costly mistakes. Unfortunately, this is not always the case, and many clients come to us in pain because their existing network is performing poorly, and they're not getting the responsiveness or the performance they need. Time is money, of course, and if their employees and network users are sitting around not being productive, it's not healthy for their business. That being said, the simple question, "What are you trying to accomplish?" is where everything starts, regardless of whether we are building out a new infrastructure for you, or if we have been engaged to remediate infrastructure which is already in place.

The answer to the "What are you trying to accomplish?" question is essentially the seed to the Pre-Design phase, the time to make a checklist and answer some key questions. To the point of this chapter, the first could be, what are the business apps being leveraged in the cloud? Next, is there VoIP (Voice-over-Internet Protocol)/Video/Unified Communications in place or on the horizon? Is your environment PC, Mac, a mixture of both, or are there other Operating Systems? What compliance standards is your business required to maintain compliance with? How are your users working today, and how will this adjustment be integrated into the day-to-day company operation?

4. A MATTER OF VOICE?

A key component in any design is what VoIP or Unified Communications Solution needs to be supported? Unified Communications systems are being delivered via the cloud with a blazing set of advanced features enabling efficiency and mobility like never before. An example of being "Unified" is when the office voice, mobile voice, video conference, instant messenger and your email are all in a unified system so no matter which you use, they all work seamlessly together. Unfortunately, email is not always efficient for real time conversational communications that are necessary in running a day-to-day business. Have you ever had a conversation in email, where the threads splintered off and multiple conversations which are difficult to follow spread throughout a email string? People take email for granted, but it is a 20-year-old technology and the traditional protocol is a bit outdated for real-time contemporary communication. Instant messaging fills this void, and today goes a step further by providing a users status, or "presence." One of the things that modern instant messaging can help with is informing team members that someone is currently occupied or on the phone. It's a way to know when a teammate is available for a question or conversation without walking down the hall, or calling without success. For our purposes, understanding where this application lives and the path to get to it, is critical. We will talk more about the path later.

The Pre-Design phase dictates a certain way that we will tune a network to support the voice and video component, which matters a great deal from a quality of service perspective.

5. LOCATION! LOCATION! LOCATION!!!

The next question is, How many locations and where? This means the physical locations and where they are located. All of these details are designed as part of the overall solution that includes Internet connectivity and setting up networks to help clients get their applications in the cloud.

In determining the system's location design criteria, it's also important to consider the following key

questions:

- How many users will there be at each location?

- Is there existing ISP connectivity?
- Are there existing assets like existing network equipment that might be serviceable or need to be maintained, like a switch or a router?...let's keep going down the checklist...
- What is the client's tolerance for downtime?
- How long can they afford to be offline?

The thing with cloud applications is when you lose your connection to the Internet for any reason; you really learn how dependent you are on data. When I say downtime, I'm talking in the sense that it becomes a factor in your budgeting. More reliable connectivity of course has a higher cost than, say Broadband, which is also high speed but doesn't have the same level of "uptime." "Downtime" means that when there is an outage, and your phone and email don't work, how many employees can you afford sitting around doing nothing while waiting to be back online? How many customer calls can you afford to miss? These questions cannot be underestimated.

What we in the IT solutions business do is, present clients with options. Clients can get a hundred mbps fiber Internet connection for $2,500 a month, or a cable connection for $300 a month. That's a $2,200 difference, but the fiber connection will rarely ever go down, and cable can go down for hours at a time frequently. So that's where it becomes a question of – What's your tolerance level? And, is it worth it to pay extra money for a more reliable Internet connection?

6. WHO ARE YOU, AND WHY SHOULD I LET YOU IN?

Ok, you've made the decision to put resources in the cloud, great. Now how are you going to manage them? Are you going to manage usernames and passwords for every cloud application? Of course not, so some form of centralized authentication is in order. Most refined cloud providers today will integrate with clients' AD (Active Directory) Servers, and yes, those can live in the cloud too! This functionality will allow users to authenticate to their own local active directory server. When we say AD, we mean that users authenticate to their own company authentication server, which becomes a central administration point for cloud services. The cloud service then queries the client's active directory server for validation of the client trying to access it.

7. MORE PIECES TO THE PUZZLE

Now we get to, what are the client's in-house support capabilities? Do you need an internal help desk to help your users and assist with applications, troubleshooting and general IT support? If yes, companies like ours can provide this service, so if something is not working the way expected, clients can call and the challenge is resolved. The overall design is a reflection of the client's needs. Other considerations are the ISP, or ISPs plural, if a client has a low tolerance for downtime, in which case we can use redundant Internet connectivity and even use two Internet providers. The next piece of the puzzle is the CPE (Customer Premise Equipment), including the network, router, switch, firewall and WAP (Wireless Access Point). As with other elements of the system, the quality of those devices is directly correlated to the experience and cost. If you want things to run like a Ferrari, you have to have the budget! The selection of the right components will directly affect the quality of everyone's experience using the network.

Our experience has been that for cloud apps to really perform the way we want them to, you have to have an impeccable network, and when we have that, we're basically giving those packets the best opportunity for success – because everything is as impeccable as it can be on the LAN so the only variable is the public Internet. With a well-designed cloud provider and impeccable network, the uncertainty of the public Internet impact is reduced.

8. A FEW MORE CONSIDERATIONS

So what about your AD server? Do we put the server on the

network to facilitate authentication? That's up to you and your computing resources. Users can use their own devices or a scaled-down workstation because the application is really living in the cloud. Phones are one of the things we'll also look at, because if they have VoIP phone, we have to think about whether we need to use a POE (Power over Ethernet) switch. Subnet consistency is also crucial because if a client has multiple sites, we're going to use an IP addressing scheme that is consistent across the site. Making the whole thing run is the UPS, or uninterrupted power supply, which provides the power for the network router, firewall and land and VoIP phones.

9. MANAGEMENT AND MONITORING OF THE CLOUD

Once we design and integrate the system, the last piece is really the care and feeding, or management and monitoring. That's where we have the high-end network tools that measure the health of the network connectivity from the user to the cloud app. What that does is allows us to see the performance of the network and help the client isolate issues or items that are not performing as expected. We can then provide remote management. Part of our management and monitoring services is a configuration backup – so that if a device fails, everything is backed up so it can be restored with a minimal amount of downtime.

Our tools help us measure the integrity of the ISP service level agreements (SLA). So if you buy a 20 mg Internet connection and you're only getting 15 mg on average, the ISP is still charging you for 20. Our monitoring tools will be able to show that discrepancy. We can't fix it but your ISP can, and we hold them accountable on your behalf. Most business owners don't know that this can be monitored. Once they're aware they like the idea that they're always running up to speed and getting what they pay for. We basically become the client's advocate to make sure the services are being delivered correctly. We're very big on fundamentals and believe that everyone should get what they pay for.

10. WHAT NETWORK IS MY APPLICATION ON, AND WHY DOES IT MATTER?

Previously when discussing VoIP and UC, we talked about the path. In data terms, we are referring to Peering, which is the voluntary interconnection of separate Internet networks for the purpose of exchanging traffic between the users of each network. Who your ISP peers with, from a network perspective, to the backbone provider, and ultimately the network where the cloud applications live, will have a direct correlation to the user experience.

For example, I live in Northern California, and want to drive to New York City. To keep this simple, let's say there are two options, I can drive Interstate 80 nearly the whole way, or take the side streets all the way to New York City. The interstate is going to be much faster with a uninhibited path. Side streets will be riddled with red lights, stop signs, bus stops, and frequent directional changes. When you think about driving coast-to-coast on the Interstate versus side roads, there is a clear benefit to the Interstate. This is essentially an analogy of your data and how it reaches its destination, and what is best accounted for during the design phase. Peering is the relationship your ISP has to its upstream backbone, how you are connecting to the net – and the path to your applications.

We all like to think of the cloud as a happy place that we can access anytime, anywhere and will always give us a stellar experience. But those who put their apps in the cloud without thinking about the hard details of how to get there might be in for a bumpy ride. The people that don't lay the correct groundwork don't understand that if you don't have a good network and a strong, uninterrupted Internet connection, the cloud is not really that happy a spot after all.

About Robert

Robert Boles is the Co-Founder and President of BLOKWORX. Robert brings more than 14 years of solving real business challenges for clients, ranging from individual, family-owned businesses to Fortune 500 corporations. Robert's core belief in Security, Reliability, and delivering a Positive User experience drives BLOKWORX's fundamental practice of building scalable, secure, IT Solutions that users enjoy working with.

Prior to founding BLOKWORX, Robert was an Enterprise Systems Engineer for an international communications company providing Advanced IP services based on Cisco, Juniper, HP, and Checkpoint, among others. Robert was a highly-specialized engineer, one of only four in a company of over 200,000 employees. Robert worked cooperatively with Product Marketing, Sales Organizations, and Operations to create a suite of managed service offerings, and defined many of the processes and technology selected within the projects. Then, as a Systems Engineer directly supporting the sales organizations, Robert designed, successfully implemented, and seamlessly transitioned to the support team over 100 managed network solutions for clients among over 1,400 global locations. As a subject matter expert, Robert educated clients, engineering, and sales teams on the Advanced IP product portfolio, which consisted of Wide Area Network Services, Network Security Services, Colocation and Advanced Hosting.

After 7 years with the company, Robert made the decision to go back to his roots, and create an IT service provider which met his vision. BLOKWORX was driven from the start to solve real business challenges with technology, by delivering modular, secure, scalable IT Solutions for its clients. Given BLOKWORX's exceptional client retention and long-term relationships, the formula is working.

Robert was raised in Arbuckle, CA, a rural, agricultural town outside Sacramento. His father was a local businessman, and his mother managed the local bank. Following high school, Robert joined the United States Marine Corps and served in Operation Desert Shield/Desert Storm. This early-life experience impressed upon Robert the value of relationships, doing right by people, and teamwork. Lessons which, in application, have fueled the BLOKWORX philosophy that, "If we always take care of our clients by doing right by them in the most honest way, having fun in the process, then everything else will take care of itself."

A featured speaker for both internal and client presentations and events, Robert is widely valued for his integrity, passion for technology, and ability to solve business challenges. Robert lives in San Francisco, CA with his wife Sarah, son Jack, and dog Chewie.

BLOKWORX is a member of the National Veteran Owned Business Association (NaVOBA), and proudly supports CompTia Troops to Tech.

More information available at:
www.blokworx.com
http://www.troopstotechcareers.org

CHAPTER 8

IT PROS: ITAR CONTENT

BY SEAN DANIELS

Today's supply chain is global in scope. With growing frequency, manufacturers, engineering groups and service providers find themselves supplying and sourcing internationally, and organizations exporting products and services for the Defense sector encounter complex regulatory challenges. The International Traffic in Arms Regulations (ITAR) and Export Administration Regulations (EAR) are a series of controls imposed by United States regulatory agencies for the restriction, tracking, auditing and oversight of the exportation of defense-related, classified and "dual-use" items. More information about these regulations are published at:

- http://gpo.gov
- http://www.pmddtc.state.gov/
- http://dtic.mil

Organizations subject to the ITAR/EAR need to navigate a complex series of restrictions. This chapter provides generalized compliance guidelines related to information systems, specifically. Your compliance officer should retain the services of a qualified ITAR/EAR consultant to assist with the design and implementation of a customized plan for your organization.

DIFFERENCE BETWEEN ITAR AND EAR

The ITAR imposes restrictions and controls on the export of defense/ military-related products, subcomponents, technical data and services. These "Items" are placed on the United States Munitions List (USML) overseen by the US Dept. of State, Directorate of Defense Trade Controls (DDTC).

The EAR differs from the ITAR in that it imposes controls on "dual-use" items that have both a commercial application as well as a military application and are placed on the Commerce Control List (CCL) overseen by the US Department of Commerce, Bureau of Industry and Security (BIS).

PENALTIES AND NON-COMPLIANCE

Organizations and individuals failing to comply with these regulations are subject to significant civil and criminal penalties. Regulated organizations must be able to demonstrate that a valid compliance program has been implemented and undergoes periodic self-auditing. Penalties are severe:

- Personal/corporate fines up to $1,000,000.00 per violation.
- Criminal Penalties up to ten years imprisonment per violation.
- One incident can incur multiple violations.
- Loss of export privileges (Debarment).
- Seizures/impounding.

Violations are published in the State Department document *Ongoing Export Case Fact Sheet.*

TECHNOLOGY CONTROL PLAN

ITAR/EAR-regulated organizations need to draft a Technology Control Plan (TCP) which includes policies for the control of Technical Data and its accessibility, transport and disclosure. The TCP defines policies, procedures and protocols to ensure compliance. This section discusses the TCP as it relates to an information system that contains or processes Technical Data.

TECHNICAL DATA

Placing controls and restrictions on Technical Data requires knowledge of what qualifies as Technical Data in your organization. Properly identifying Technical Data is critical to keeping it secure in its various forms (digital, paper, at rest, in transmission, in discussion, etc.) and in assessing/auditing internal processes.

Paraphrased definitions of Technical Data from Department of State and the Department of Defense (DOD) are provided here. Be sure to work with a consultant who can further define the definition as it relates to your organization.

Department of State (ITAR)[1]:

- Classified information relating to defense articles, technology and services that includes research, design, development, integration, manufacture, testing, repair and refurbishment.

- Information covered by an invention secrecy order.

- Specific software required for development, production and use of defense articles (defined in §121.8(f)).

- Excludes:

    a. Marketing publications and events disclosing only basic information about the general function, purpose or system descriptions of the defense articles.

    b. Information in the public domain (defined in §120.11);

    c. General academically-taught design principles.

    d. Securely encrypted, unreadable data not decrypt-able by key disclosure or other means. Once decrypted, it is again

---

1. EAR & ITAR Technical Data Definition Harmonization available as:
   plenary_May2013_TechDataWhitePaper.pdf

controlled under the ITAR.

The Department of Defense (Document 2040.02)[2] offers a similar definition plus:

- Technology that advances the state of the art, or establishes a new standard, in a significant US military application.
- It exists in tangible form, such as a model, prototype, blueprint, photograph, plan, instruction or operating manuals.
- Or in an intangible form, such as a technical service or oral, auditory, or visual descriptions.

FOREIGN NATIONALS

The ITAR/EAR restrict the intentional/unintentional disclosure of Technical Data to foreign nationals. A TCP needs to impose the isolation of Technical Data in any form from operational processes, electronic storage or transmission and physical areas accessible to foreign nationals or unauthorized personnel. Foreign nationals are anyone except:

- A U.S. citizen or lawful permanent resident
- Certain refugees to the U.S.
- Individuals granted U.S. asylum

TCP AND COMPLIANCE IN IT

Consider the following guidelines when protecting Technical Data in your system and workplace.

DIRECTORY SERVICES

Directory services (I.E. Microsoft's Active Directory Service) can be leveraged in securing Technical Data. Consider organizing the directory in a manner that makes resources containing technical data easily identifiable and inaccessible to unauthorized individuals

---

2. http://www.dtic.mil/whs/directives/corres/pdf/204002_2014.pdf

and foreign nationals. Separate domains or sub-domains might be created to further separate classified data and authorized users from the rest of the organization. Logging services, organizational units, group policies, security groups, password polices and workstation restrictions should all be invoked to ensure the security of Technical Data.

INCIDENT RESPONSE PLAN (IRP)

An Incident Response Plan should define a rapid-response procedure to sever all access to Technical Data should a breach be detected and throughout subsequent forensic measures and investigation. The procedure may include creating a snapshot of servers or a compromised computer at the moment of detection. Work with your consultant to define the process for responding to such attacks and drafting an ERP.

TWO-FACTOR AUTHENTICATION

While important to maintain strong passwords in your environment, consider invoking 2-factor authentication, allowing a second layer of authentication, often in the form of a One-Time-Password (OTP). The OTP is unique to the moment of time the user is logging in. Formerly available via tokens, fobs and smartcards, systems today can provide OTP via smartphones.

SSL-ENCRYPTED WEB PORTALS

Ensure that users are aware of the difference between securely-encrypted web sites and those that are not. Train users on such best practices as:

- Ensuring sites requiring passwords have addresses beginning with HTTPS

- Ensure the validity of SSL certificate protecting each site

- Open secured sites manually as opposed to clicking emailed hyperlinks

DATA RETENTION

ITAR/EAR regulatory agencies mandate a data retention period of five years for any data and documentation relevant to the export of regulated items. Discovery processes need to produce data and documentation demonstrating ITAR/EAR "items" were delivered to their intended final party and the route taken. Your consultant will help to identify records necessary to the ITAR/EAR. Retained records might include documentation vetting customers, shippers and freight forwarders, employee/contractor background checks and citizenship verification records, and downstream Automated Export System (AES) transaction records.

Technical Data backups should invoke DOD-approved encryption standards before leaving the premises. Cloud-based backups must perform on-server encryption before transfer.

DATA DESTRUCTION

It's extremely important that regulated data or documentation be destroyed properly. If, after the mandatory 5-year retention period, destruction is desired, invoke DOD-approved data sanitization and destruction methods to ensure Technical Data is properly destroyed on such media as:

- Disks and portable media
- Server storage
- Decommissioned workstations and laptops
- Discarded documentation
- Copiers: Internal hard disk storage
- Tablets, smartphones and digital devices

Outsourced data destruction services offer approved methods of data and document destruction, and they often provide a *Certificate of Destruction* as proof for your records.

THIN-CLIENT COMPUTING

A primary goal of regulated organizations is improving security through the reduction of the *Vulnerable Surface Area* of networked infrastructure. The *Vulnerable Surface Area*, a measure of the exposed vulnerabilities existing across the computer infrastructure, should be minimal so threats have significantly fewer targets and services to exploit.

Fully-functional operating systems like Microsoft Windows, MAC OSX and Linux, allow applications to run locally on workstations. Vulnerabilities are often discovered that require patching on a regular basis. A network of computers running fully-functional operating systems offers a significantly large *Vulnerable Surface Area*.

Minimizing the Vulnerable Surface Area often includes deploying thin-client computers. Running a limited operating system with no local data storage or significant vulnerabilities to exploit, security is significantly enhanced. Additional benefits are: (i) reduced cost-of-ownership and (ii) a consolidated administrative model.

CLEAN COMPUTERS FOR TRAVEL

Users accessing Technical Data while travelling should be issued a laptop computer or mobile thin client that contains no Technical Data. Maintain an inventory of these *Clean Computers* on standby for check-out and check-in by traveling personnel. Each computer should be inspected and cleared before being issued and should be inspected, quarantined and sanitized upon return.

If these units will display Technical Data, attach privacy filters to the displays that limit viewing from individuals who are not directly in front of the screen. Technical Data should not be displayed in areas of uncontrolled surveillance or those accessible by foreign nationals and unauthorized individuals.

REMOTE ACCESS

Accessing technical data remotely should, at minimum, require the use of a securely-encrypted channel of communication such as a VPN connection. Two-factor authentication is also recommended such as a Pre-shared key or SSL-encryption plus smartcard, RADIUS or One-Time-Password (OTP).

PORTABLE MEDIA

Ensure that portable media such as USB or Flash storage is encrypted and tamper-proof. Many such devices invoke DOD-approved encryption and can self-destruct when challenged. Some offer enterprise management capabilities.

EMAIL TRANSMISSION

Email, inherently one of the most insecure methods of messaging, should invoke:

- Automatic TLS encryption with supporting sending/receiving servers.

- Policy-based email encryption systems which inspect message contents and automatically encrypt those that contain Technical Data.

- On Demand email encryption allowing senders to manually trigger encryption.

- The ability for an external recipient to reply in an encrypted manner.

- Policies regarding authorized recipients.

- Disclaimers stating your organization's policies prohibiting the unsecured email transmission of Technical Data.

SOCIAL ENGINEERING

Efficient hacking organizations often mine for information about target organization and its users on the web, social media and via telephone and email conversations. They'll effectively use this information to deceive users into divulging information that leads to a breech.

Educate users on such best practices as not publically posting employee information to social media or in telephone conversation with unfamiliar individuals. Everyone, from receptionists to security officers and end-users should be well informed.

EMAIL AS AN ATTACK VECTOR

Technical barriers such as IDS and firewalls can be easily defeated when an employee is duped into acting on a dangerous email. A common technique to gain access to protected data by hackers is the Spear Phishing attack. Through social engineering and other research, hackers tailor email messages to look legitimate and familiar to internal recipients. Acting on such an email may disclose a user's credentials or give computer control to remote hackers. Educate users on such best practices as:

- Dragging suspicious emails to Junk Mail to disable attachments and disclose true hyperlink addresses
- Hovering the mouse to reveal true hyperlink targets
- Submit attachments to IT personnel for inspection

INTERNAL WI-FI NETWORKS

Internal Wi-Fi networks should be designed to isolate resources hosting Technical Data from those that don't. Deploy centrally-managed wireless access points that offer multiple secure SSIDs for different purposes such as ITAR, non-ITAR, guests, presenters, etc. On production SSIDs, implement enterprise-level authentication such as 802.1X, EAP and RADIUS protocols or managed, per-device keys. Invoke strong encryption such as WPA2. Require visitor registration on guest Wi-Fi through registration portals or guest management.

Non-production Wi-Fi networks need to be segregated from internal information systems and offer only Internet access. Adopt Wi-Fi technologies allowing on-demand access-revocation of any device, and consider the use of a logging server for auditing or emergency response purposes.

TOPOLOGY SEGREGATION

Ensure conference rooms and areas accessibly by foreign nationals, visitors and/or non-ITAR individuals do not offer data ports/jacks that will place an unauthorized device on the same network as Technical Data. Data ports should be documented and configured to allow or deny access to Technical Data resources. Shared ports should invoke the use of VLANs and the 802.1x port authentication protocol to authenticate the connected device and provision the appropriate type of access. Simpler LAN topologies may provide a physically separate switch attached to a DMZ port on the firewall for conference room and visitor data jacks.

SECURING PORTABLE DEVICES

Regulated organizations should secure and manage integrated mobile devices. Consider the following:

1. Issue company-owned smartphones and mobile devices to travelling employees.

2. Deploy/enforce policies and restrictions on portable devices via Mobile Device Management (MDM) technology.

3. Use MDM to restrict which Wi-Fi networks to which devices may connect, restrict applications installation, prohibit personal email, perform Remote Wipe procedures and enable location tracking services.

4. Prohibit the devices from connecting to unsecured or public Wi-Fi hotspots.

5. Encourage or require the issued smartphones to be used as

mobile hotspots for Clean Laptops instead of third party Wi-Fi.

6. Prohibit the use of personal smartphones and mobile devices for business use, from containing corporate intellectual property, Technical Data, employee directories, employee email, etc.

TRADE SHOWS AND EXHIBITORS

Any computers, portable media or data devices to be used at trade conferences or expositions must not contain Technical Data. Slide shows or presentations should be approved by management or compliance officers to confirm they contain no Technical Data or classified information. Information provided via presentations and exhibits are categorized as "Transfers" and are thereby regulated as follows:

• Typically deemed "permanent" transfers and require DSP-5 permanent export license for slide show presentations and associated technical information.

• Securely store computers and digital media to avoid theft.

• Present using clean, secure laptops with disk encryption and minimal data content.

• Use caution when disclosing information. Remain conscious of data that is public domain and data that is regulated.

• Protect your organization by obtaining a Marketing License in advance. Clear the presentation and scripts with the Office of Security Review (OSR).

CLEAN DESKS, CLEAN MEETING ROOMS

Designate secure areas where meetings discussing classified data take place and classified documents are processed and reviewed. Ensure that no video conferencing equipment, microphones, web cams, smartphones, multimedia devices, etc. are installed or allowed in those

Clean Meeting Rooms. Ensure Clean Desk areas offer locked storage for sensitive documentation and portable media.

FACILITY ENTRY

Procedures for facility access should include a sign-in requirement and badge issuance. Foreign nationals should be identifiable at all times by badge color or other attributes. Consideration should be given to a system that takes an electronic photo of visitors, stores the data and prints a color-coded badge with legible photo to inhibit badge swapping.

INTERNAL VIOLATIONS REPORTING

Provide a dedicated email address or web portal for internal employees who wish to confidentially report violations of company policies. The email address might forward to the compliance officer. Ask employees to provide their contact information in the communication, and be sure that the officer receiving the message has the ability to respond with action items.

CONCLUSION

In this chapter, we provide very broad guidelines to consider in several key areas of IT as they relate to the ITAR/EAR. Your system may require different or additional measures. Complying with the ITAR/ EAR requires close collaboration with a qualified expert consultant who can assess your organization's unique requirements and create a compliance program specific to your needs. Organizations must demonstrate that a proper program is in place and is undergoing regular auditing and improvement. It is not recommended to implement a "canned" approach possibly found online, as penalties are severe for violations that these shortcuts may leave exposed.

About Sean

From his first experience programming in high school, Sean Daniels always had a keen interest in computers. He later studied scientific and business-oriented programming languages like FORTRAN, Assembler and C++ in his college years at the University of Massachusetts, Dartmouth, where he earned a Bachelor of Science in Electrical Engineering in 1992.

Sean formed his first computer services company the following year and began pursuing certifications with major industry partners like Cisco, Microsoft and Novell. He has since been consulting in a wide variety of industries including automotive, aerospace, athletics, education, financial services, warehouse management, distribution, non-profits and legal with major emphasis on health care and manufacturing.

In 1998, Sean created NetSoft, Inc., a software development company and IT Pros, its IT services group. Dedicated to providing a complete portfolio of services to clients of all types and sizes, Sean and his team designed and executed solutions ranging from custom software design to IT security and business continuity. In subsequent years, NetSoft would design software for a well-known collegiate athletics conference, national non-profit organizations and large health care groups, while IT Pros would build and support the datacenters that hosted those solutions.

As Managed IT Services became a more mainstream offering, IT Pros incorporated it into its services portfolio. This fixed-fee service model presented clients with a predictable monthly fee for IT services, and its success led IT Pros to later introduce a similar plan where clients were provided hardware and software as part of the monthly service fee. This Hardware-as-a-Service program is now one of the hottest products in the portfolio and has helped IT Pros to distance itself from its competitors.

Sean and his team's proudest achievement is building a successful technology services company based solely on referrals since the nineties, cultivating a loyal client base resulting in hundreds of successful projects. Quality people providing quality service has been the key to this successful growth, caring about client success every step of the way.

In 2010, for his efforts in expanding collaborative technologies for non-profit organizations, Sean would be awarded *Partner in Philanthropy* of a national non-profit organization as well as an honorable mention during a *Governor's Award for Service to Rhode Island* ceremony presented by then governor, Donald Carcieri. Today, Sean continues to conceive IT solutions to provide a more efficient and cost-effective collaborative operating model for non-profit organizations.

Sean's expertise in healthcare technology has earned him a seat on the Board of Directors of a prominent Management Service Organization since 2008. During his tenure with this Board, Sean has directed efforts in EMR development, federal guidelines, datacenter and Software-as-a-Service design and deployment, technology adoption and onboarding. As of the date of this publication, Sean still serves at the pleasure of this Board and the MSO executive officers.

To connect with Sean:
Email: sdaniels@itpros.us.com
Phone: 1-855-777-7891

CHAPTER 9

FIVE CRITICAL REQUIREMENTS FOR DATA BACKUP

BY TOM CROSSLEY

In the 1980's I started a property management company, overseeing more than 250 residential units. At that time, everything was done by hand. We had dozens of green ledger sheets for rent rolls, wrote over 150 hand-written checks per month and manually balanced over a dozen checkbooks.

Within a couple of years, I had my first experience with computers and found, with my engineering background, I was quite adept at this new-found technology. We put everything on an old pre-DOS PC and, for the time, it was quite revolutionary. The checkbooks balanced themselves! I was saving a ton of time every day and I felt the freedom to abandon all the manual paperwork that seemed to consume most of my workweek. Life was definitely good – UNTIL the hard drive crashed. Back then no one even thought about a hard drive crashing. But it did!

Now picture in your mind a young man picking up the telephone to call tenant after tenant (all 250 of them) asking, "Did you pay your rent this month?" Followed by, "How about last month; do you owe anything from last month?" To this day I don't know exactly how much money I lost as a result of the hard drive crashing, but I know it was many, many thousands of dollars. And that was just the beginning, I spent a year and countless hours trying to piece back together all my lost data. I never fully recovered, but fortunately, I was able to stay in business. However, that is not always the case when there is a catastrophic data loss.

Consider these staggering statistics related to lost data for today's companies:

- "93% of companies that lost their data for 10 days or more filed for bankruptcy within one year of the disaster, and 50% filed for bankruptcy immediately." (Source: *National Archives and Records Administration* in Washington)

- 20% of small to medium businesses will suffer a major disaster causing loss of critical data every 5 years. (Source: *Richmond House Group*)

- About 70% of business people have experienced (or will experience) data loss due to accidental deletion, disk or system failure, viruses, fire or some other disaster. (Source: *Carbonite*)

Don't become a statistic! By implementing the following five key points you will be able to mitigate your risk of data loss and potentially even save your business.

FIVE KEY POINTS THAT ARE MINIMUM REQUIRE-MENTS FOR ANY BACKUP SYSTEM

To protect your business, you need a reliable backup system you can count on when you need it. The minimum critical key features required are; onsite storage for minimal downtime, offsite storage for redundancy, server virtualization to have usable backups, cloud server virtualization for protection from catastrophic events, and monitoring and testing for verification.

1. Onsite Storage
Onsite backup consists of some type of local storage, usually a hard drive, where your data is periodically backed up.

When your backup is onsite you can typically restore a file in minutes. However, if you are totally reliant on offsite or cloud backup and you have to restore a large file, or possibly all your data, because you had a catastrophic failure, keep in mind that it will take as much time to get the data back down to you as it did to get it offsite in the first place.

A lot of businesses use nationally-branded cloud backup systems. A typical business may have hundreds of gigabytes or several terabytes of information. It can take anywhere from 3 to 5 weeks for that information to be totally uploaded offsite to the cloud. Not all that time is due to bandwidth restrictions; some of it is due to the vendor throttling how much you can send to their servers because they have thousands of clients with whom they work. The point is this, if it takes 3 to 5 weeks to send the data up to the backup provider, it will take that long to restore it.

Can you realistically wait 3 to 5 weeks to have all your data restored from that service? Even if it's only a 10-gigabyte file, can you wait a few days? The question is, how long are you able to survive without your data and what will the downtime cost you? Onsite storage, on the other hand, enables you to recover that same data in minutes.

NOTE: STAY AWAY FROM TAPE BACKUPS! They are simply not reliable. Hard drives are the best way to backup your data onsite.

2. Offsite Storage

Offsite storage means getting your data out of your building – usually to a qualified datacenter (aka "the cloud").

While there are time issues inherent in offsite storage, it is also a critical part of a robust backup system and is something that can't be ignored. If you have a catastrophe in your office, such as a fire, equipment theft, employee sabotage, etc., you may very likely lose your local backup. If the fire doesn't get to your onsite backup, the sprinklers will. To protect all the data that could be permanently lost in a catastrophic event, your information must also be stored at an offsite datacenter.

Choose your data center carefully. Their job is to keep your data safe and available. A good data center will have redundant locations with state-of-the-art security. Within each location they will incorporate redundant systems such as multiple power sources, multiple data connections coming in from opposite ends of the building, and other factors that mitigate their risk of downtime. In fact, their uptime rates are typically 99.999%.

3. Server Virtualization

Most backup systems only backup your data. However, you are risking significant downtime unless you're backing up your server's programs AND data (as well as the security settings, VPN, remote access, printers, user logons and everything else you rely on your server to do). The data is of no use without the programs to access it. To illustrate, if your laptop crashes and you have a backup of your Word document, you can recover the file. But, if you don't have the Microsoft Word program, that Word document does you no good. That's an easy example to understand, but it gets more complicated when you have other line of business systems you must restore.

The reality in business is that there will be times when servers crash. Hardware fails. Although servers usually have built-in redundancies for power supplies and hard drives, there are components that are not redundant (i.e., mother board), or there may be multiple failures. I've actually seen smoke coming from a server! In addition to hardware failures, a server may crash due to the operating system becoming corrupted.

A server is not something you can buy at your favorite local office supply store. A server is a long lead-time item that must be ordered from the manufacturer and built to your specifications. Then, once you get it, there is significant time to get it set up. The point is that if your server goes down and you're not prepared for it, you could be without your data for 3 weeks or more.

Most people in business have heard the term "virtual server." This is a server that runs all the functions of a server, but does so without having its own dedicated physical box. A good backup system will capture an image of your entire server and, when required, will also be able to run your business on a virtual server giving you access to all the data, programs and settings of your own server – in minutes, not weeks.

At 11:30 one morning, I received a call telling me the system was down at one of our best clients. At the time, I was out of state helping another customer. However, I was able to remote into the network. I spent 28 minutes trying to resolve the problem with the server with no luck. At that point, I decided I was not going to be able to fix the problem remotely and even if I was onsite it could not be resolved quickly. So, from that same Internet connection into their network, I remoted into their backup device (which was backing up 4 different servers) and was able to spin up a virtual server from the backup device which emulated everything verbatim – of the original server that crashed. It took me 4 minutes to spin up the virtual server and I was able to call the customer to let them know they were up and running again.

The users didn't know they were operating off the backup device because it was a seamless transition. They had everything back and were able to work as usual. The employees didn't even know their server was dead. It was a total of 32 minutes from the time I received the call to the time they were back up and running. If we hadn't put the appropriate server virtualization backup measures in place, this would not have been possible.

Another benefit to server virtualization, although not critical, is called "bare metal restore." Because the entire server image is captured on the backup device, if you have to replace or reformat the hardware, you're able to take that backup device and push the image back to the server.

In the instance where I was out of state and had the business back up and running within 32 minutes, we went to the customer site at about 6 that evening. The problem with the server ended up being corrupted operating system files – the hardware was OK. We just needed to rebuild the server. Because we had the ability to do a bare metal restore, we ran a cable from the backup device to the server and restored the entire server – programs, data, settings...everything! What could have taken us up to 40 hours to rebuild, we were able to complete in 3 hours with a bare metal restore. So, they had their own server back when they returned to work in the morning.

4. Cloud Server Virtualization

Cloud Server Virtualization is the process of pushing a copy of the entire server image to the cloud. This is extremely important under certain conditions. For example, in the Northeast a couple of years ago, due to a huge storm, power was out in some communities for more than 2 weeks. If a business is faced with a disaster such as this (or tornado, flood, fire, etc.) they'll have the ability to go to a different location that has power and Internet, rent office space, bring in some laptops, and set up a VPN to the service provider that is storing the cloud backup. With this they can actually run their programs with their data just like they were in their own office. By doing this, we can set up an entire remote office in half-a-day, and get a business back up and running in a different geographic location. Assuming you can get personnel to a different location, through cloud server virtualization we can get your business back up and running within a few hours because everything you have in your office we have in the cloud.

5. Monitoring and Testing

I can't stress enough the importance of monitoring and testing your backup systems. Obviously, in order for your backup system to be effective you must make sure it is fully functional. The following example illustrates how important monitoring and testing are to the success of your backup systems.

I received a call from a panicked business owner last September. She explained that her files were encrypted and she couldn't open them. I suspected the CryptoLocker virus. She was using another IT company at the time and explained that she was dissatisfied with them and now her files were encrypted. She wanted me to come to her office immediately to help her.

When I arrived she and the internal IT person were standing in front of the server just watching files get encrypted. Their IT company was remoted into their server trying to stop the bleeding. When they brought me up to speed I told them to unplug the server from the network immediately. Their response was, "No, we can't. Our IT guy is working on it." I explained that the attack was most likely originating from a computer on the network and repeated, "Unplug the server." She then called her IT guy and was on the phone with him for about five minutes. Meanwhile, folder after folder was getting encrypted. Data was being destroyed as we watched! She finally came back and we unplugged the server. We were eventually able to determine which computer was the originator of the attack and were able to mitigate the effect of this vicious virus.

Now to the point: They had a backup service in place. They had gone for quite a while without needing to restore anything and had become complacent about their backup. No one was watching. After we were able to stop the bleeding from the CryptoLocker attack, we needed to restore their files. We went to the backup service, found the folders we wanted to restore, but discovered that the backup had not been working since April. That was 5 months previous to this incident! No one was monitoring the backup and there was no notification from the backup company that the service was interrupted. The end result was that this business lost 5 months worth of files. To make things worse, they were in the middle of an IRS audit. So, the loss of these files became a very serious problem with far-reaching implications.

This real life incident is a prime example as to why you need to monitor and test your backup systems. If you rely on one person to make sure the backup activity is taking place on a daily basis, you are setting yourself up for failure. You need to know without any doubt that your backup system is working continuously. Monitoring and testing are critical.

Warren Buffet said, "What the wise do in the beginning, fools do in the end." That is a truth that applies directly to backup systems in IT. If you can't learn from the mistakes of others, you do so at your own peril and at the peril of everyone who counts on you. A good backup system is one of the most valuable and least costly business insurances you can get.

The "Five Key Points that are Minimum Requirements for any Backup System" discussed in this chapter are recommended as "minimum requirements." It's not OK to have three out of five or four out of five. You must have all five of these strategies in place to safeguard your data.

If you don't have these things in place, I encourage you to find a qualified MSP to help you protect your data. Not only will it potentially save your business, but also it will protect the jobs of your employees and the valuable service you provide to your customers.

About Tom

Tom Crossley is an Information Technology support expert who is passionate about delivering technology that "just plain works the way it's supposed to." Tom is founder and president of Fairoaks Consulting, Inc., bringing world-class, enterprise-level IT support to small and medium-sized businesses for over 20 years.

Technology advances at a dizzying speed. While technology helps small to medium-size companies, it also frightens them as they can't afford the infrastructure to actively adopt the newest and best, nor to defend themselves from the constant threat of being invaded or outdated. For a fraction of the cost, the small to medium-sized company can have all the benefits of a large company's in-house IT power from Fairoaks. Their motto, "You Manage Your Business. We'll Manage The Technology Behind It." sums it all up.

Tom prides himself in providing personal service. Distinguishing themselves from a large IT chain's off-the-shelf service, Fairoaks staff knows their client's business, their names and their unique situations. They enlarge and empower small companies. Tom's ethical stand is "I treat my client's money as if it was my own." There is no one-size-fits-all service. All of his clients' IT needs are crafted to align with their business and their budget. "I have to be creative to give them state of the art, essential and affordable service and I'm proud of it." says Tom. Many business owners are proud to add Fairoaks to their 'My Doctor, My Financial Advisor and My IT Guy' list.

It's Tom's strong belief that the success of small to medium-sized companies is the key to strengthening our nation's economy. Because of this, he enjoys sharing his expertise with other business owners speaking on data security, network management, business continuity and other topics at live events, radio broadcasts and webinars.

Tom graduated *summa cum laude* from the University of Massachusetts in 1979 with a dual degree in Industrial Engineering and Operations Research and a minor in Industrial Psychology. Before applying his practical, no-nonsense approach to the IT arena, Tom worked for GE as a consultant and manager throughout the U.S.A., the Caribbean and Asia, then co-founded a property management company in Massachusetts.

Tom brings his dedication and focus to his personal interests. He is an avid, instrument-rated private pilot who also has a passion for invention. In 2010, Tom patented a new product for a portable, off-airport aircraft tie-down system, and along with his son, Adam, co-founded Storm Force Tie Downs. The product has been sold at trade shows and online since 2011.

Away from the office, Tom likes to spend time with his family, getting away to the cabin in Maine for some hiking or snowmobiling. With his family, Tom has hiked and camped from the canyons of Utah and Arizona to the Swiss Alps and Italian seacoast. He's also been known by his friends, on a clear morning, to extend an invitation to fly with him to Martha's Vineyard, landing on a small grass airstrip for breakfast at the airfield before work.

You can connect with Tom at:
Tom@FairoaksConsulting.com
www.LinkedIn.com/in/TomCrossley

CHAPTER 10

YOU CAN TAKE IT WITH YOU: THE FUTURE OF MOBILE COMPUTING

BY JUSTIN LENKEY

CLEARING UP THINGS: MOBILE COMPUTING DEFINED

In a business world dependent upon real time response, mobile computing is imperative to success. Yet misconceptions surrounding mobile computing continue to persist. Many people use the terms "cloud computing" and "mobile computing" interchangeably, but they are very different things.

Essentially, mobile computing offers users the ability to use wireless technology to connect to, and use, information systems and software that are centrally located through portable communication devices. With mobile computing, your data is accessible wherever you are. If a company desires its employees to utilize mobile computing, then it needs to invest in mobile hardware and software that allows an employee to take a device and all necessary files or software into the business field. Three of the main classes of mobile computing are:

- portable computers, such as laptops, notebooks, etc.

- mobile phones, including cell phones, smartphones and PDA phones.

- and, less common now but anticipated in the near future: wearable computers like jewelry, keyless implants, etc.

The existence of these last devices is expected to be long lasting and complementary in terms of personal usage, none replacing the other in all features of convenience.

We can simplify all of this information by saying mobile computing is having your data with you wherever you are. This is different from cloud computing which is the practice of using a network of remote servers hosted on the Internet to store, manage, and process data, rather than a local server or a personal computer. While cloud computing can be utilized in the practice of mobile computing, it's not necessary. Nor does cloud computing only exist for the purpose of mobile computing.

Perhaps the simplest way to introduce the concept of mobile computing is by showing examples of it from daily life. The GPS found on our phone or dashboard is a form of mobile computing that connects to a remote computer network and determines where we are and where we are going. If we get pulled over for a ticket, the police officer runs our driver's license via a remote computer in his car that can access records anywhere at any time. These are forms of mobile computing that many people have grown accustomed to in daily life. These same concepts can be successfully applied in the business world to enable an organization greater ease and functionality.

DOWN TO BUSINESS

Many of us may be familiar with basic mobile computing and how it impacts our personal lives. However, the benefits of mobile computing in business should not be minimized. Having mobile access as a corporate resource can allow direct interaction with data from systems at work via tablets, laptop or phone. At the very least, this minimizes downtime experienced by business travelers.

Ten years ago, this sort of access took place over a slow wireless connection, if it was available at all. At the time, remote computing was confined to slow systems such as dialup. Now most devices are equipped with LTE, or Long-Term Evolution, commonly marketed as 4G LTE, which is a standard for wireless communications of high-speed data for mobile phones and data terminals; with higher speed came greater communication possibilities. Today, a business traveler can edit actual documents, create presentations, analyze reports and hold or attend face-to-face meetings in addition to accessing email. Most of these activities can be completed on tablet devices, which are smaller to travel with than laptops, though even laptops have shrunk to a fraction of their original size.

The explosion of tablet computing shifted the paradigm for those who find writing part of their day-to-day business. From a tablet device you can access centrally stored clouds, but not all devices will connect to clouds. Some connect to business applications, such as accounting software, human resources, or manufacturing data that connect to remote corporate servers, but not clouds.

A good example of this are the devices used by courier services like UPS and FedEx for electronic signatures. When you sign your name on those devices, your signature transmits back to the company's main servers to track packages and update data in real time. The main servers relay information and display it back to the driver remotely. This form of mobile computing is gaining popularity in major retail businesses and grocery chains alike. Vendors servicing retail stores use mobile devices in their aisles to complete remote inventory. The employee captures sales and inventory statistics on these handheld devices and sends them back to a central computer; one not located in the store, but in the vendor's facility. Then, the vendor can make informed decisions about which products to stock in a particular store and how effective product placement is.

With food products, companies often have a consigned inventory. Inventory control employees are sent to stores with smartphones to scan bar codes on the shelf so they know what needs replenishing and what the store's bill should reflect. For example, if there were ten jars of peanut butter last week on the shelf and only three now, the store is responsible to pay for the seven no longer there. This is accomplished utilizing a phone app.

Traditional retail mobile computing predominately uses a gun-style bar code scanner. Unfortunately, there are only a few manufacturers of these devices and they cost thousands of dollars each. Compare that to a smartphone or tablet that is only hundreds of dollars, and it's clear that mobile computing is and will continue to dramatically change the standard of how such devices will be used in the future. Companies can no longer consider completing inventory with pencil and paper methodologies. As prices decrease and technology becomes more affordable, it makes sense to develop real-time solutions for inventory and warehouse management. Mobile computing now allows many industries access to inventory and sales needs – anywhere and at anytime.

Keep in mind, however, that despite these overall trends, larger stores forgo smartphone application use to a particular point. Many major big box retailers use internal mobile computers that double as phone devices to allow associates to talk to one another while having a bar coding solution built into it. It's not a smartphone obviously, but a phone designed for internal usage that provides a multitude of functions. It can be used as a phone within the store's network, a stock locator device, and can be used for mobile customer sales. So why opt to provide specialized devices to employees over a simple smartphone app? The device is a better solution for their company needs. Upgrading technology to mobile devices will usually allow retailers to offer greater customer service, better inventory control and improved software management for a small investment. All of this offers a great return on investment for the organization implementing this form of mobile computing.

THE MOBILE COMPUTING/MOBILE COMMERCE LINK

As with anything in technology, mobile computing and mobile commerce are rapidly evolving areas. One piece to this puzzle was the arrival of virtualization platforms almost a decade ago. Virtualization software and hardware allow a single host server to run one or more computers. This allows for greater flexibility within a business.

Generally speaking, when discussing virtualization with our clients, we want our customers to be more agile, responsive and profitable. Currently, virtualization software packages are transforming how businesses and technology providers work and collaborate by taking the traditional office environment and enabling it on any type of device. We recently took accounting applications and made them externally available for organizations on tablets and other devices, and also wrote native software for smartphones and other devices. These were not cloud apps, but applications that communicated with a company's existing infrastructure in real time.

So what does the future of mobile computing look like? Currently, people have real time access to corporate data. It's accessible anytime in any location so that they are not limited to one central location. However, there are still larger sources of data that are unable to be seen on a smaller screen; this portion of mobile computing will continue it's expansion as limitations on what can be accomplished while traveling will continue to diminish.

Many companies are increasing their efficiency and decreasing costs by utilizing logistical mobile computing. Many organizations are able to streamline their operations by using apps and devices to track deliveries and locate remote employees in the field. The trucking industry understands the benefit of this technology. Twenty years ago, trucking companies started using technology to keep mobile logs and track their fleets in real time; allowing the organization to make better fuel cost estimates. Now, as more developments in mobile computing are made, this technology has become more affordable and companies are switching from conventional satellite tracking to mobile computing. This allows better route planning, more accurate cost analysis and greater profit. The goal is to take technology used right now and record transactions and review data where it's needed, which isn't necessarily where it lives.

Mobile payment services will continue to emerge as a cost effective method of commerce. Mobile commerce is more than just buying items from an app on your smartphone or on the web from your laptop. Emerging technology will allow a consumer to use a computerized device in a store and check out as items are added to a cart. Several chain stores are currently pioneering this technology. This concept naturally extends to a smartphone app that allows customers to scan items as they shop and then complete the sale on their phone through a virtualized wallet such as PayPal or Google Wallet. The convenience and efficiency of this technology is appealing to customers and retailers alike. Mobile commerce even has the propensity to eliminate stressful holiday shopping situations. The downfall is that older populations are hesitant to embrace technology, especially when it concerns virtualizing their banking and payment options. Mobile commerce is hindered by a lack of trust in security and is further injured by data breeches such as those experienced in the 2013 Holiday Season at multiple retailers.

ASSESSING MOBILE COMPUTING DRAWBACKS

Far too often, companies look at newer technologies, see the benefits that are offered by incorporating those solutions into their daily business, and jump to the conclusion that changes must be made quickly to stay competitive in their industry. As with any major decision that affects all areas of business, a company should also assess and understand the negative areas of mobile computing. This isn't to say that the following concerns are "deal breakers" – instead they are areas that require discussion before successfully implementing mobile computing. Discussing potential drawbacks to mobile computing allows a company to proactively educate employees and attempt to create solutions to customize mobile computing to their individual organization's needs. By being aware of these common pitfalls, a company can enjoy greater success while incorporating mobile computing into its day-to-day business practices.

SECURITY ISSUES

As with every issue related to cyber communications, mobile computing has vulnerabilities and security issues. There are probably hundreds of pages of information that can be found related to keeping data safe, but for the purposes of this chapter, I'll outline basic concepts to consider when increasing mobile business capabilities.

In general, make sure that when dealing with any apps, you are only exposing information you want exposed. Remember that the network your organization works on daily only maintains Internet security. That means that if an employee is working on a public network at a local coffeehouse, others using that network can access the information they are working on. A business utilizing any IT company or department that is competent can easily secure their private network, but no such guarantees exist in the outside world.

A security breach is one of the largest possible threats to a company, and when data is externally accessible, there's always the danger that it can be removed (even accidentally) or accessed by someone who could compromise it. Taking security measures into consideration early in the implementation of these processes is key. Security features can be as simple as educating employees on mobile computing practices or as complicated as investing in encryption software. A company's needs and the types of mobile computing utilized should determine how to proactively secure data. For some companies, security fears are a major deterrent to switching from paper to digital transactions. They shouldn't be. IT companies, like ours, can be a valuable source of information on how to safeguard your mobile computing environments.

LIMITED COVERAGE AREAS

An area of great frustration when working remotely with data is the quality of coverage from the local Wi-Fi provider or cellular service. While an organization can plan well and have a solid wireless infrastructure, there is no guarantee that a mobile workforce will encounter the same quality. For this reason, it's important to choose apps that can work based on your needs. When collecting data, a company should look for an app that will collect the data with or without immediately connecting to a network and will upload the data when connectivity is re-established. The most valuable applications will store information in the memory of the mobile device and upload it later.

A good example of this is a mobile time clock used at construction job sites. Many of these applications work with or without cellular data connectivity and will upload all data as soon as an Internet connection is available. A couple of years ago, I worked with a company of mobile sales representatives and seed brokers. They regularly visited agricultural companies and wanted to electronically take orders; alleviating their need for paper. Unfortunately, their cellular signals often did not work in the middle of a farmer's field. By thinking through the obstacles in their way and understanding what they ultimately needed in order to successfully complete their job, we found an appropriate software to make sure the process would work with or without network coverage. Part of working in the IT world is coming up with effective solutions for unique situations. After all, technology only benefits a company when it works the way it needs to work. Before assuming that all applications or software packages will fit the needs of your organization, it's important to evaluate what all of your needs are and then carefully analyze whether or not each solution is a good fit. Simple planning eliminates frustration later.

STILL WORTH IT

In the end, a company's desire to engage in mobile computing comes down to increased worker productivity – and in general, the potential benefit from implementing these solutions pays for itself thousands of times over. When working with a mobile network, the productivity gain should be derived from being able to make real time actionable decisions from anywhere. The physical constraints that used to limit business functioning are eliminated. In many instances, mobile computing is part of a larger software package that a company implements to maximize profits and efficiency – though IT service companies can create independent systems when necessary. In today's business world, companies should make mobile computing a strategic part of their future endeavors.

About Justin

Justin Lenkey helps his clients extend the functionality of their technology and fully maximizes their investments. He does this with the idea that technology does not have to be overly complicated to the consumer, and therefore, is dedicated to help his clients understand their technological investments in plain English. Over his career he has worked with a diverse range of clients in various environments including healthcare, food processing, petrochemical, manufacturing and transportation and logistics. All of Justin's clients are given personalized solutions that are created with industry-best practices in order to improve their business systems.

As an expert in Enterprise Resource Planning and warehouse management techniques and practices, Justin is able to improve operational efficiency and help his clients better serve their customers and stay competitive. He regularly offers continuing education events to his clients that are designed to enhance each user experience in the products they invest in. Ensuring that IT and business solutions produce solid results has never been more critical to the longevity and success of an organization. By focusing on proactive maintenance, security and infrastructure solutions and custom applications, Justin can collaborate with individual companies in order to ensure the success of their partnership.

Justin is founder and Managing Partner of Argyle IT Solutions; a leading IT services provider that works in relationship with Fortune 1000 companies. Argyle focuses on increasing business productivity by managing and supporting both Hardware and Software while offering a single point of contact for any issue a company might have. Dedicated to being an extension of a company's IT team, Argyle continues to support and educate their clients beyond the scope of a traditional IT services provider. The customer must be successful in order for Argyle to consider their project successful.

CHAPTER 11

TELECOM

BY JOHN KILLCOMMONS

Business communications is driven by two operative words: simple and reliable. However, when it comes to telecom, businesses often have very simple problems and they overcomplicate the solution. They will go out and buy a very expensive system, which has every bell and whistle. I find it fascinating that a company may spend hundreds of thousands of dollars on a PBX or phone system and 95% of their users will simply use the system as a plain old telephone.

In this chapter I will outline some key considerations when making decisions about the telecom needs within your organization. Since telecom is such a broad subject, we won't be able to cover every facet. But, the following information will serve as a solid guide when trying to identify your basic telecom needs. When deciding how to provide quality phone service to your business or organization, you must begin with some very investigative questions.

WHAT FEATURES DO WE NEED?

The specific features you will need are driven by a few factors such as the number of users in your organization, the type of business you conduct and your budget. However, for the most part, the following features are the most commonly used by businesses.

Direct Inward Dial numbers or DIDs – DIDs are **virtual numbers** that allow you to route calls to an individual or group within your organization. This feature was developed to give companies the ability to assign certain employees a direct **number** without requiring multiple physical phone lines.

Voice Mail – In today's environment of technology everyone expects voice mail to be a very common feature of any phone and it is vital to the efficient operation of any business.

Notifications – If you are away from your phone or your office, this feature allows you to receive a "notification" message by email/SMS indicating you received a voicemail message in the office. Some notification systems will also attach the voicemail to your notification.

Interactive Voice Response system or IVR – This feature provides a recorded message with instructions on how to reach certain individuals, departments or extensions by utilizing the telephone keypad or by speech recognition.

Call Recording – Recording calls, both incoming and outgoing, helps the overall business quality assurance and provides a mechanism to train and evaluate your staff. It will also serve to keep your employees on their toes and is very useful for training opportunities as calls are monitored.

Call Details Records or CDRs – Your phone system should have the ability to produce reports that will enable you to know if you are functioning at a level of efficiency. For example, you may want to know things such as how many calls were placed and received, the duration of each call, how many calls were dropped, how long it took for a call to drop, ring-to-answer rate, etc.

Auto-Receptionist – This feature enables a business to set up a professionally recorded greeting that welcomes their customers then the call can be routed according to the established protocol. Typically, if no one is available, the caller will be sent to a voicemail and the voicemail can then be delivered to the assigned person immediately to respond to the call.

<u>Music On Hold</u> – Music On Hold is a nice feature to keep customers entertained while they are waiting to be transferred or on hold for another reason. It also gives the caller an assurance that their call has not been dropped. When a customer hears nothing, they may think they have been disconnected and may terminate the call.

<u>Group Extensions</u> – There is often a business need to have an extension for an entire group within a company. For example, a Customer Service group may be made up of a dozen or over one-hundred users. This feature enables the caller to be connected to the Customer Service group and any number of people will be able to answer the call and provide the appropriate service for the customer.

<u>Caller ID</u> – Caller Identification or Caller ID can be beneficial to businesses for many reasons. It enables you to screen calls if necessary, be more prepared for the call by knowing who is calling, or simply capture a phone number in case a call back is necessary.

<u>Intercom</u> – The intercom feature enables one person to reach another phone within the same office by pressing a single button. Phones can be programmed to intercom certain extensions that are more commonly used.

<u>Paging</u> – Paging enables someone within the telephone system to send a page or attempt to reach a particular person within the phone system.

<u>Conferencing</u> – Conferencing allows multiple people to be on the same call at the same time within the same phone system as well as externally.

WHAT PROVIDERS ARE IN YOUR BUILDING CURRENTLY?

This is a very important question and one that is often overlooked. Know what providers are currently in the your office building. This will help you receive better service and overall will reduce the cost of securing both Internet and phone services from the provider. There isn't anywhere you can find published information about what providers are available in specific locations and buildings so you will have to go to the building owner or management group to obtain that information.

Most buildings will have the Incumbent Local Exchange Carrier (ILEC) located in the building. However, it may be in your best interest to find if a Competitive Local Exchange Carrier (CLEC) or a cable company. If you don't have a CLEC then you are limited in your choices of services. Please don't run your business on a DSL connection, especially if quality is a concern. I don't ever recommend DSL for business applications. Instead, I would recommend going with cable or FIOS as they provide plenty of bandwidth and the service is generally better. Cable providers do face an issue if the network is shared among multiple businesses within your area. For example, if you and 10 other businesses purchase a 30 Mbps Internet service but the building is only serviced with a single 100 Mbps pipe out of the building, you may not get all the capacity you want at a given period of time since other users are also accessing the same service. However, in general, cable companies are good about upgrading the service capacity when congestion points in the network are found.

Network diversification will assure that your phone and Internet systems are always up and running. The best method to ensure network diversification is to have two network access providers. If, for example, you only have the ILEC in your building, you would use a wireless solution like LTE (Long Term Evolution Technology) to provide your backup network service. Please select a router that would automatically monitor your two network providers and switch you over automatically in the event of a network outage on your main provider. There are several options available to accommodate this scenario. Some businesses choose two facility-based providers and one wireless provider. That way, from a network connectivity perspective, you're connected and you have failovers in place.

Your Internet network connection is important, especially if you are moving your phone service over to an SIP-based phone provider.

HOW MANY PEOPLE ARE IN YOUR ORGANIZATION

Are you a 10-person organization? 50-person? 100-person? If your business has more than 100 people in the organization you will need serious bandwidth. If that is the case, you are more than likely spending between $2,000 and $3,000 per month on network services at each location. You will want to check with your local cable and CLEC to see if they will bring fiber services into your building. By doing this you will save money and increase the quality of the service.

Unfortunately, people don't usually think about their options with respect to network service providers. However, you should always look for alternative providers to your location and don't hesitate to reach out to the cable provider(s) in your area to see if they will come into your building with the same or better bandwidth at the same price. Also keep in mind that you can negotiate with providers. The ILEC generally will not move off their pricing but CLEC/cable providers are more flexible and truly want your business. Show the higher-priced provider what their competitors are offering and see if they will match or beat the competitor's price.

Generally, 1 to 5 user businesses are usually very simple and can get away with cable phone service. They can get a set of 5 phones at their local office supply store, wire them in, and that should meet their general needs.

For companies with larger phone needs, from 10 to 50 phones, it makes a lot of sense to incorporate a hosted phone system. This will give you service and platform upgrades as part of the monthly cost of the service. It also gives you the ability to incorporate your phone service into your businesses disaster recovery plan.

Companies from 50 to 250 phones are great candidates for a hosted phone solution, especially if they are multi-location. At this level you really need someone that understands your phone platform and the specific needs of your business and is able to customize it accordingly. I have one customer who created a new company but wanted to use the same phone number. So, we took their phone platform, did a lookup on their database, and when we saw an inbound call coming in, we were able to match it and route the call to the appropriate group. So they were able to get a very specific customization to their system without having to pay a great deal of money for an enhancement.

WHO SHOULD BE INVOLVED IN THE DECISION-MAKING PROCESS?

Having the right people involved when making choices about your telecom needs is extremely important. You always need an executive "champion;" a person from the executive team that will be highly supportive of a viable solution to the company's telecom needs. You should also include the person(s) responsible for the IT staff/ firewall/ and network; the security manager; and make sure the accounting department is involved.

It's also helpful to get perspectives from different people within the organization as to what current phone issues exist and to understand what they would like to see in a new system. In these meetings users have the opportunity to disclose telecom issues that management may not even know exist. On the other hand, on occasion I have discovered in these meetings that the organization really doesn't need to upgrade their phone systems. The end users also help you determine the features necessary to carry out their responsibilities as well identify the "nice-to-haves." So, you can see these types of interactions can be very important in the decision-making process.

HOW MUCH SHOULD I PAY FOR A PHONE SYSTEM?

You will find there is a very wide price range in the telecom industry and sometimes you will discover you could have purchased the same phone system for half the price. However, in many instances, people tend to buy the cheapest, but they usually sacrifice quality when they do.

When comparing pricing, you should look at cost per handset and ask the PBX vendor to give you a cost per handset. As a rule of thumb, once you get above $500 per handset, you're probably buying a lot of stuff you don't need; that price includes the actual physical phone, all the software, the service to run it, and everything else it takes to make the phone functional.

It is not uncommon for a business to purchase a carrier's services, but never audit the provider's invoices. Most often, people don't understand these details and allow the communications provider to charge them without a complete understanding of the charges. It is important for companies to question their bills and challenge the carrier to keep the pricing as low as possible; regardless if you are under contract or not, this should be done.

HOW DO I STAY UP-TO-DATE ON THE MOST CURRENT TECHNOLOGY?

Let's face it, you have a business to run. Unless your business is telecom, it is unlikely you will be able to stay abreast of the ever-changing nature of the telecom industry. The best thing for you to do is to get connected with a trusted telecom professional who will monitor and evaluate your telecom needs on a regular basis.

There are constant developments taking place in the telecom market as it relates to business. Advancements are consistently being made and new applications abound. One of the introductions to the market is a cutting-edge technology I have developed that unifies all communication in and out of a company. It enables you to do SMS, web portals, video, audio, video/audio conferencing, recording, and transcribing from one platform while being very stable with very low balance requirements.

For example, a user can receive a text message from a mobile device to this platform on a PC that is dropped into a queue. The PC user is then able to text message back to the mobile phone user through this platform. This application can be used in a diverse number of business verticals. To further illustrate, if an EMT picks up a patient with a trauma wound, the technician can take a picture of the wound with their phone and text it to the Trauma Center triage nurse, so he/she knows what to prepare for the arrival of the patient to be able to treat them in the most efficient and effective way. The call can then, if necessary, be escalated to an audio or video call to the doctor. An evaluation of the patient can possibly be made prior to their arrival at the Trauma Center – which could save critical and potentially life-saving minutes.

This system is a consolidation of communications, which allows the user to use audio, video and text messaging on an all-secure platform. This can also be connected to Sugar or Sales Force platforms. There is nothing to install on your PC since everything is pushed from the cloud. Since this is all web-based, if a software update is implemented, you don't have to install a patch on multiple machines. Instead, the next time a user logs in after an update, they will have the most up-to-date version.

There will always be emerging trends in the telecom industry. The best way to stay up-to-date is to connect with a telecom provider you trust and who is also staying current through continuing education. As with any specialty field, trusting the right expert is a very important factor. When you find that professional they will serve you well and help you take your business to new levels of efficiency and productivity.

About John

John Killcommons is an IT Expert and entrepreneur whose professional goal is to build lasting relationships and to coach and train others to become experts. John's clientele ranges from small medical groups to a Fortune 500 company, primarily focused in the greater Bethpage areas.

John's dedication to innovation is shown by his Patent for modifying and routing DICOM examination files (US: 11/6277779) which are used everyday in the medical industry. This has been directly tied with work he has done with his brother to design and develop products for MedWeb. John also is a leader in setting direction for the Medical and communication industry and provides support for the reliability, security, quality and affordability that makes PixelRiver and Medweb the industry standard for distributed telemedicine and teleradiology solutions.

John graduated from SUNY Maritime with a B.S. in Electrical Engineering and a U.S. Coast Guard Third Assistants Engineers License for any steam or motor vessel in any ocean. After graduation, John took a job with Exxon Shipping Company until1996, leaving as a First Assistant Engineer and traveling the globe. John secured a position with MCI Local Service as Technical consultant where he helped to build out 90 local phone markets following the telecom act of 1996.

John held a number of positions with MCI, WCOM, VzB and lead teams of engineers to build out the largest VoIP network of its time generating $1.2 billion for MCI. John was the director of professional services for NightFire – a small Oakland, CA company that developed a business rule validation platform with service provider interface which allowed all CLECs to place orders with all the major ILECs. The platform would validate the ordering process for number ports and facility-based services.

During his extensive professional career, John also took time to help develop a few private businesses, including Nexsys Electronics, Inc, Medweb, PixelRiver Technology, LLC, and RadiologyRecords, LLC. These diverse and very successful businesses provided a number of software and IT solutions to both private companies and governments around the world.

John has recently turned his passion and experience with building technology businesses to areas of personal interest – most notably, Globalcall.com providing high end VoIP solutions and conferencing, and SportsFoundation Development Group to support the consulting requirements of the sportsfoundation.com.

Learn more about John at: www.pixelriver.com

CHAPTER 12

HOW TO INCREASE OUR PRODUCTIVITY, EFFICIENCY AND GROWTH OF OUR BUSINESSES THROUGH IT
– WHILE ACHIEVING 40% SAVINGS ON BUDGET

BY SIMON FONTAINE

TECHNOLOGY – A NECESSARY EVIL?

Technology is there to help us **make our work easier, be more efficient and achieve our business objectives**. Why isn't that the case for most people I meet? Why is this **a puzzle, a necessary evil and a money pit?**

For most business leaders, technology is not a priority and they have more important things to do. They have no desire to be *IT* techs, and have great difficulty in navigating the complex language of technology. They have no other choice but to trust their supplier and technical resource they hired to look after their *IT* - and they feel they're already paying too much. Unfortunately, many of them still have bad experiences. They regularly hear the same speech about efficiency and productivity in *IT,* but they never reach their intended goals.

As a leader, you know that you need to invest in technology to stay in the race. But if you do not have the expected returns on investment, it remains a cost to you.

Why did we get there?

Why is *IT* still seen by many as a necessary evil, a source of stress and a significant cost for businesses?

As businesses become increasingly dependent on technology, their services and the amount of data continues to grow in addition to their importance. The dependency ratio in technology has grown exponentially over the past 10 years. We only need to look at business leaders and their tolerance to fault and data loss in *IT.* These emergencies highly contribute to their level of stress.

Yet they have the choice to capitalize on technology rather than remain victims...

Facts:

1) We are investing more and more in technology, and the services they render us are more and more critical to our business.

2) We have no other choice but to follow the evolution of technology. If not, we're overtaken by the competition.

3) Many articles touting the successful use of technology appear every week.

Why, with all the promises that are made, doesn't technology deliver the goods?

HOW TO GUARANTEE 100% RESULTS?

– Define the role you want to give your *IT*: convenience or strategy?

If you choose convenience ...

Unfortunately, this is still often the case in business - dealing with problems one at a time, fixing crises and emergencies on the fly. We buy reactively when the need arises because of the absence of overall vision.

Projects are often approved without global overview. We are given a false sense of economy through expenditure control in choosing what intuitively seems to be the best cost to benefit ratio. But in fact, we're just going around in circles.

The consequences? We try to go forward with one foot on the gas (want more sales, more market share) and one foot on the brakes (*IT* spending cuts), a vicious cycle that inevitably causes a slowdown. *IT* becomes a ball-and-chain to businesses when it could be propelling it.

Then comes the day when the company "hits his wall." Systems are down for several days, there's a loss of data and there are budget overruns on projects without gain for the organization. The company resource holding all information related to *IT* leaves the company. There are bad purchases and bad technology choices, outdated environment and significant technological gaps.

Business leaders then ask themselves if there is another way of doing things...

Have you ever truly evaluated the real costs associated with this chaotic approach where *IT* is an expense?

I'm not talking about free-spending here, but rather what will bring the most value to the company. As leader, you make decisions on what has the most impact for your business. You want every dollar you earn to profit and support your business plan.

Choose the strategic role to support business growth:

As a decision maker, you want the best **cost/benefit** ratio. You want to invest in *IT* services that will bring the most value to your business, and which will help you achieve your financial goals.

HOW TO KNOW EXACTLY WHERE TO INVEST IN *IT* IN THE NEXT THREE YEARS

To do this, you must:

1. Invest in the TOP 3 *IT* services that will support your business plan. These services must be reliable and adjusted to your business reality and needs.

Examples of services include: sales, customer service and production/ ERP software, interactive websites, IP telephony, email, etc.

2. Make these services more efficient and more effective and align them with your business plan.

Prioritize ONLY high gain projects that are aligned with your business plan – those that bring value to your business.

Let's explore in more detail the two items mentioned above:

1. Invest in the top 3 IT services that will support your business plan.

You must first indentify these services because they are the ones that contribute not only to ensure the quality of your customer service, but also have an important impact on the operations of your business, and therefore your business results.

Otherwise, it's hard to ask that your employees be productive and efficient if these services are unstable, slow and inefficient! It's hard to sell your product and services if you do not deliver on your promises.

This is where we assess the costs versus benefits to maintain the stability of these services. To help us make the best choices of which projects to put forward, it's helpful to perform an exercise to evaluate the financial impact of an outage versus the cost that different solutions can represent.

Benefits:

The benefits are to avoid financial losses due to the impact on operations and on all customers, as well as the emotional impact on management, customers and employees (stress, dissatisfaction with the performance of *IT*, instabilities, etc.).

Quantify the financial impact on your business if these services are deficient (such as breakdowns, delays) to assess actual harm to your organization. For example, for a manufacturing company, downtime can cost $10,000 per hour. The financial impact represents profits or stability and efficiency.

In this case, how many hours of downtime can you tolerate? Is your current technological environment able to respond?

Costs (the cost to implement the solution if needed):
Example 1: System outage of production/ERP software per hour

Duration of the outage Tolerated	Financial impact on the business	Cost of investment (solutions)
1h	$10K	$100K
8h	$80K	$20K

An eight-hour disaster recovery solution is different from a one-hour solution and will not have the same cost or the same impact.

Your decision will depend on the amount you are willing to invest versus the risk of impact on your finances. Are you willing to invest $100K to ensure that you're back up and running in an hour?

You want to make the best cost/benefit decision. If instead, you choose to invest $20K, you'll be back up in 8 hours. You just set your level of fault tolerance that will increase from 1 to 8 hours given the costs of the solution.

Calculating the cost/benefit ratio:

The previously outlined process should have made it possible to evaluate your cost/benefit ratio.

Costs/Benefits: $20K / >$80K

You now have all the tools to properly define your projects with measurables: Your goal is to avoid subjecting your business to an impact of more than $80K per failure, the cost to implement the solution is $20K and your tolerance level is 8 hours.

Example 2: Data Loss
When addressing the subject of the protection of corporate data, the majority of business leaders are confident of what they have in place, and they feel safe. In reality, after an audit, **nine out of ten companies fail the test**. The result? When a problem occurs, they realize they do not have what it takes to get back up quickly.

The first question to ask yourself is: what is the real value of your data (incl. production logs such as orders and inventory, as well as data such as sales funnels and customer lists, etc.)?

Case 1:
Here is a real-life example of an evaluation performed with a database of blood tests belonging to a researcher in the field of health. Each test costs $500 per person for a total of 2000 people over a period of 25 years. Also, consideration must be taken for grants and subsidies allocated in the amount of $200K/year over that same period.

- Evaluate the database value: ($500/test x 2000 people) + ($200K x 25) = $6M.

This data is critical because it's impossible to rebuild quickly. The estimated $6M represents a minimum value.

- Estimated cost of a backup solution: $10K/year.

- Ratio = (Cost/Benefit): $10K/$6M = important because of a high risk level.

The impact of losing all of the company's data is high, so the level of tolerance for data loss will be very low = 0/10.

Case 2:

System down for 3 days, unrecoverable data loss estimated at $45K, $15K per day.

- Estimated cost of a backup solution: $9K/year.
- Cost/Benefit: $9K per year/$45K loss =

Payback is a half-day. Risk of failure of a half-day in the year was high (8/10). The solution pays for itself in half a day.

- Level of tolerance = ½ day.

In case of data loss, how many days of work are you willing to lose? You could, for example, decide to tolerate a half-day because the cost of the solution is minimal. Whether it's retrieving files or complete data loss, we always want to calculate the ratio = (cost/benefit) to know the impact before choosing a solution.

As a business leader, you want to make decisions on what really impacts your business. Your must invest your time in the right places. Your *IT* department is probably the last thing on your mind when it should be the first. Here's a solid example of this: The evaluation of the data value represents a task which cannot be delegated. Here's why:

Compare three departments: production, administration and *IT*. Let's calculate the financial impact if each department manager is not doing his job properly.

1) An error in the production department may shut down production temporarily, causing **a loss of $10K to $100K in revenue**.
2) An error in the administration department, such as a lost invoice or check: **a loss of a few thousand dollars.**
3) An error in the *IT* department, such as incorrect critical data backup (ERP, payroll, legal documents, etc.): **a loss of a few thousand dollars up to bankruptcy.**

If you really want to invest in the right place, you should do this exercise with the top three essential services that you have identified, for the following four components:

1) Fault tolerance

2) Tolerance for data loss: erroneous deletion of a database, loss of a quote, loss of email, complete loss of business data (Acts of God)...

3) Performance level: slowness, inefficient software...

4) Security Level: cost of downtime for five days after a virus attack, data theft, etc.

This whole process will serve as a benchmark for each *IT* investment.

Now that we have made these services reliable and adjusted to your business needs, we want to make them effective, efficient and align them with your business plan. Is this the case now? If not, what improvements need to be made?

2. Align technology projects with your business plan to turn them into a lever.

Use your strategic business plan and complete this exercise with each of your projects. Invest in *IT* projects with high gain that will bring value to your business and build a powerful tool to propel your organization.

Example: Inventory turnover improvement project.

We want to go from a 4 to a 6.5 turnover rate. We want to reduce the inventory 15% to 20%. The estimated benefits are $1M and the cost of an *IT* solution is valued at $50K.

Costs/benefits: $50K/$1M

Payback: the solution pays for itself in 2 weeks!

Do this exercise for all your business projects to find the best ratio.

SELECTING AND PRIORITIZING PROJECTS

Now that we've pinpointed stabilization and optimization projects that will bring value to the company, we have to prioritize the ones with the most potential ROI and take on one at a time and see each one through to its succesful completion, and build each project on the success of the last one.

You must also consider the following elements:

- The level of urgency.

- The impact of not achieving them.

- The challenges.

- The efforts of internal and external resources.

- Who will manage the project and will be held responsible for its delivery.

You now know exactly where to invest, how and why. You can start focusing on high gain projects that will bring value to your business.**

FIVE KEYS TO SUCCESS

1) <u>Change your perception and adopt a strategic role</u>. You have much to gain!

2) <u>Upper management must be involved</u>. Take the time to do the exercise. It will be well invested in important decisions that represent a huge potential.

   Form a Strategic Committee - talk strategy, rather than technology - and an executive committee for implementation. Some decisions cannot be delegated, like the strategic role that you want to give *IT* and how to measure the assessment of the value of your company's data.

3) <u>Measure and quantify</u>. Start with the three essential services. What improvements or what can be achieved? Be specific and consider the financial and emotional costs. It's from what you measure that you make your decisions. If it's not well

defined, you will probably make a wrong decision.

4) <u>Get the consensus of all members of management</u> – President, General Manager, VPs, CFO – for all projects that you want to put forward. This will create a synergy that will make the project successful. Above all, do not take on 10 projects simultaneously! Select 3-4 projects to put forward and build on their success to create a positive impact in the company.

5) <u>Ask for guaranteed results rather than product warranties!</u>

What's in it for you...

1) You have just used technology to support your business plan and created a leverage effect. You have a stable work environment, efficient and productive, and technology is aligned with your business objectives.

2) You are in control and now have a clear vision of where, what, why and how to invest in *IT* for the next three years.

3) *IT* is now a profitable expense that brings increased value to your business.

4) Improved opinion of *IT* from your employees, more pleasant work environment, better customer service and better business reputation.

5) When purchasing a business, assessing the status and performance of the *IT* environment will greatly contribute in increasing or decreasing its value.

Real life cases
A. **Beauce Atlas,** 150 employees, specializing in manufacturing and installation of steel structures.

The company has improved its productivity and achieved a savings of 40% on its *IT* budget in 3 years. By investing its *IT* budget wisely. They've made their staff more efficient and productive. Now, 90% of their *IT* budget is invested in improvement projects and 10% in maintenance.

B. **Cote-du-Sud School Board**, 60 schools, 3,000 users.

The School Board met its educational mission and achieved a savings of $1.5M on an *IT* budget of $2M. The priority is to first meet the educational mission and to use computers for this purpose. The project was bold because there was a technical challenge. The issue was performance. The School Board is now a model for its peers who have also begun to implement the solution.

CONCLUSION

Because of its enormous potential, *IT* is probably the best strategic investment for your business. Not taking it into account would be a mistake. If you are targeting growth and efficiency, *IT* will help to facilitate your work, so business leaders no longer have a choice.

About Simon

For the last 25 years, Simon Fontaine has been a key contributor to Quebec City business owners' peace of mind when it comes to their *IT* environment. Originally from the Beauce region of the province of Quebec - an area known for the quality of its entrepreneurs - and coming himself from a family of entrepreneurs for generations, Simon has always brushed shoulders with the business world. Having a profound interest in technology, he founded his own company in 1989.

According to Simon, technology must simplify work and contribute to achieving a company's business goals. His own goal is to help business owners and CEOs achieve concrete results by taking a different approach to *IT* than what is being done presently— not to invest more, but to invest differently. As a businessman with 25 years under his belt, Simon has built a solid methodology that allows him to guarantee his results 100% if his recipe is followed to the letter. He combines his experience with specific tools, indicators and measurables adapted to each client's reality. He primarily works with businesses where *IT* plays a critical role, meaning that business results are directly proportional to their efficiency. Simon understands the importance that *IT* takes up in the business world and the impact it has on organizations.

Simon is the President and Co-founder of Les Services Informatiques ARS Inc. His business has more than 300,000 projects and interventions to its credit in business sectors like manufacturing, professional services and POS—companies ranging in size from 50 to 1000 employees. ARS is known for its ability to take on technological challenges and to deliver results.

You can get in touch with Simon at: simon.fontaine@ars-solutions.ca

** Report information to give you a quick overview: One page strategic Plan
at: www.ars-solutions.ca

CHAPTER 13

WHAT TO LOOK FOR IN AN IT PROVIDER

BY VINCE TINNIRELLO

Before entering the Information Technology (IT) world, I spent 10 years working in the hotel business. I enjoyed the hospitality industry and learned a great deal about customer service and how to treat our guests. Now as a long time IT business owner, I continuously draw on my background in the hospitality industry and make sure to place a distinct emphasis on customer service, relationship management and doing business the right way. I am very passionate about my industry, the work we do with our clients, and treating our customers with the utmost honesty and integrity. Unfortunately, I have often found this business component lacking in many IT Service Providers (ITSP) in our industry.

I know that hiring a company like mine is similar to me taking my car to a mechanic. If they tell me I need brakes, then I have to trust they are being honest with me and that I really do need brakes. My customers have to have the same trust in me and I want to make sure they continue to have full confidence in my recommendations by always being honest with them. Small business owners have to trust their IT provider, but how do they know who they can trust? Allow me to answer that question by suggesting some things you should look for to help you choose the right IT Provider.

DETAILED CLIENT ONBOARDING PROCESS

Your IT provider should have a very specific plan for bringing customers into the fold. They must do their due diligence by first understanding who the users are and what specific needs within the company will need to be addressed. This is all done through a detailed onboarding process. Unfortunately, many IT companies don't have a documented and repeatable onboarding process. Before hiring an IT company it is imperative that you know about their process, if they have one at all. Without one it can be disastrous, as there will be no clearly defined expectations for the start of the relationship.

Realistically, it takes about 30 days to get a client fully onboard. The ITSP should give you an outline of their onboarding process as well as status updates along the way. The very first thing we do is to send an engineer onsite to begin talking to users, learning what their pain points are, and documenting everything learned. We aren't going to fix anything at this point, our only goal is discovery.

I also encourage companies to have a meet-and-greet with their new IT provider's representatives and their own staff. We will introduce ourselves, our company and explain things such as how they contact us, how they submit a service request, what to expect in terms of response time, etc. We also listen to the client's employees and their concerns. This helps to set the tone for the relationship, builds excitement between both parties, and establishes rapport between the two teams. The relationship with your IT provider must be a partnership; you can't treat them like just another vendor. If treated like just another vendor then no trust is built, and without trust there is no relationship.

The client meeting is a critical piece of the onboarding process that shouldn't be overlooked. Our company will not go live and start supporting a new client until we have had an in-person, client welcome meeting. This process is paramount to setting the proper expectations and positioning the relationship for success.

PRICING MODEL

How the ITSP charges for services is a key consideration. Is it a flat fee or an hourly rate? I strongly recommend you engage a company that works on a flat fee only without any hourly billing. When an IT company charges by the hour, the client loses and the ITSP wins. The premise is that if I'm hourly I'm not incentivized to fix anything quickly. The longer the client's network is down, the more money the ITSP makes. This model also makes it very difficult for clients to budget for IT support, because it could vary from month to month.

The flat-fee model is beneficial to both the client and the ITSP. With a fixed fee, the client pays for up-time and if an IT outage occurs it affects both parties. It motivates the ITSP to maintain the network in a proactive manner and to react quickly if a problem arises. The longer the client downtime, the greater the loss of client productivity and revenue, and also the greater the loss of profitability for the IT provider – as they would be expounding unplanned resources to resolve the client's issue. This is why fixed-fee agreements are win-win scenarios for both parties. They bring both parties to the same side of the table with the shared goal of maximum client up-time.

When reviewing proposals from IT companies, I recommend analyzing the fee and included services closely. I find very often that IT companies will low ball a client with contracts that appear low upfront with a flat fee, but are backloaded with exclusions and hidden fees that aren't apparent until the client gets their first invoice.

You will also want flat-fee pricing for projects in addition to the recurring monthly services. By doing this, if a project is quoted at a fixed price and it takes longer, then the ITSP must absorb that additional cost. Unfortunately, the normal process in the IT world is to indicate a project will take a certain number of hours, knowing realistically it can't be done in that time. So, IT companies will give clients a flat-fee price based on the reduced hours, but they will also have an hourly fee added in case the job goes beyond the allotted time. Inevitably the job will go longer and the client will end up with a bill for a flat fee as well as an hourly rate for the additional time. A good

IT company should have a reasonable idea of how long it would take to complete a project, and therefore quote a complete flat fee with no additional charges.

YOUR IT PROVIDER SHOULD FULLY DOCUMENT YOUR NETWORK AND PROVIDE YOU WITH THIS INFORMATION

Many traditional IT companies don't want the customer to know their own password to their own servers and they don't want the customer to have any documentation on their own network. The thinking here is if you have all that information, then why do you need the IT company? You can see how this ties into the old hourly fee model. It puts the ITSP in a position of control with the clients feeling powerless over their own IT assets. Don't allow this to happen. When I hear of these situations, I tell prospective clients it is an act of desperation by the ITSP to hang on to their business.

At our company, we believe that this is your network, which you own. You are paying us and it is our job to document everything and there should never be any information regarding your network withheld from you. If my company were to close its doors for any reason and you had to find a new IT company, you'd be able to hand all the documentation we provided to the new IT company so they could take over. If an IT company doesn't want to supply you with all of this information, find someone else.

TALK TO CLIENT REFERENCES

I offer a reference list to my potential clients before I'm even asked. Why wouldn't I? After all, I'm proud of it and our clients can tell their story better than we can. I always ask my current customers to be honest with anyone that calls them about our services. You will want to find out from references if the IT provider properly managed their expectations and if they simply met those expectations or exceeded them. Also ask, if the ITSP can't get something done in the time originally projected, do they re-establish expectations?

WHAT TO LOOK FOR IN AN IT PROVIDER

WHAT CERTIFICATIONS ARE HELD BY THE ENGINEERS AND STAFF OF THE IT COMPANY?

Hiring someone that simply tells you they are good with computers is like hiring a doctor who tells you they are pretty good at practicing medicine but can't show you their diploma from medical school or board certification. Certifications tell you a great deal about their qualifications and also if the IT company values continuing education. If an IT company attends industry conferences, earns credentials and continuously stays updated on the ever-changing IT field, then that's a good indication they have the expertise required to guide you along the way.

Specific certifications you will want to look for include, but aren't limited to, the following:

- **CompTIA Managed Services Trustmark** – We were the 26th company nationally to receive this designation, the first in our market to earn the credential and it's imperative that your IT provider has it as well. A CompTIA Trustmark helps to demonstrate that the IT provider's business adheres to the industry's best practices. It also is indicative of their dedication and commitment to performing quality service. This is a credential you have to earn through a series of rigorous audits and reviews. When a customer works with a Trustmark holder, they've got peace of mind that the IT firm is a best-in-class service provider that has been vetted.

- **Microsoft Silver Level Partner Competency** – When an IT firm joins the Microsoft Partner Network, they receive a set of core benefits that can help save time and money when delivering services and will strengthen their capabilities, better serve customers, and build connections to reach their full business potential. It's our job to give you big business technology on a small business budget and this competency helps to ensure that.

- **Specific Engineer Certifications** – Ask what individual certifications are held by the specific IT engineers with whom you will be working – such as Windows, Servers, Office 365, etc. You will want to work with IT providers who have the staff that will be able to meet your specific industry-related IT needs.

100% MONEY BACK GUARANTEE

You will want to work with a company that is willing to give you a 100% money back guarantee. If they are not willing to do that, ask them why. My company offers a risk-free money back guarantee with a zero cancellation fee. My philosophy is simply, if you aren't happy with our service, how can I possibly ask you to pay for it? Even if we have to agree to disagree, I will refund your money if you aren't satisfied. This principle has been a differentiator for us and a core value to our business. Any IT company who believes in themselves and the services they deliver should have no problem offering such a guarantee.

CLEAR COMMUNICATION SYSTEMS

It is imperative for your ITSP to clearly communicate with you regarding who you are to contact, what response times you should expect, and other expectations related to the IT need or issue you encounter. They should be able to clearly explain the process of communication so there is never any question when the need to communicate for any reason arises. Ask the IT provider for a written copy of their SLAs (Service Level Agreements) that detail the response times the client can expect for service requests. Is it same day? 24 hour? 4 hour? This must be communicated clearly in order to manage expectations properly.

BILLING IN A TIMELY FASHION

As strange as this may sound, there are many IT companies that don't bill for months and then send the client a very large bill that they expect to be paid without hesitation. When that much time passes, the client often has to question the details of the invoice because it happened so long ago. Your IT provider should have a very professional billing system that will be consistent and accurate. Ask them about their billing process and when they invoice. You should receive your billing on the same day (or very close to the same day) every month.

WHERE DOES THE IT COMPANY RANK IN THEIR INDUSTRY?

There are specific questions you can ask a potential IT provider to determine their standing among their peers in the IT industry, such as: How credible is your IT provider within your industry? Do you have any vendor references we can talk to or peers in other cities who might be able to provide any insight as to who you are? Do you participate in any peer groups? What accolades or achievements have you earned? Where are you ranked in industry polls measuring service providers? Do your peers and competitors know you? Do you make presentations at industry-wide events and conferences? Are you considered a thought leader in your industry?

MEET SOME OF THE SERVICE PERSONNEL

Some IT companies only want to give you one account manager or technician. However, I think that is shortsighted and a huge mistake. If that person gets sick or is on vacation, then what happens to that client's account? I strongly believe our staff needs to be cross-trained to know how to support all of our clients. This provides the best scenario for clients as there is not one single person with all of the knowledge locked up in their head. I also recommend that you actually meet with some of the service personnel with whom you will be working. Find out how they plan to support you, if they plan to rotate all their staff through, if they send someone onsite regularly, and have them explain their methodology of support.

ARE THE IT EMPLOYEES W-2 EMPLOYEES OR CONTRACTORS?

I recommend that all the customer-facing, day-to-day support staff, be W-2 employees. If you work with someone who outsources their help desk, there is always a sense of disconnect between the help desk and the field staff. To provide a high level of service, customer-facing help desk engineers must be actual employees. Some companies outsource the after-hours network monitoring and back office support to a vendor who assists with resolving alert-type tickets. This is ok, as it can benefit the client greatly in receiving additional coverage hours when a small IT service provider just can't provide the manpower on their own.

By utilizing the principles outlined in this chapter, I am confident you will find a qualified IT service provider that will have your best interest in mind. When you find a provider that is a good fit for your business needs, it will be in your best interest to develop a long-term relationship with them. They will be able to demonstrate their worth by saving you time and money, increasing your efficiencies and giving you a competitive edge. Not every relationship will work out, but when you find a good relationship, stick with it and build on it. It can definitely prove to be a win-win strategy for both of you.

About Vince

Throughout high school and college, Vince worked in the hospitality industry at restaurants and hotels. It was through those years of experience where he learned how customers treat service industry people, and how service industry people treat customers. He learned how to deliver good customer service and the rewards for doing so, and also how to recognize what bad service looked like and how easy it was to lose a customer.

As a graduate of the Hotel, Restaurant, & Tourism Administration program at the University of South Carolina, Vince went to work for Marriott International for 9 years. It was here that he learned how to earn customers for life, how to empower employees to care for customers, and how to communicate with people in the business world. After 15 years in the hospitality industry, Vince took his passion for technology and combined it with his hospitality and customer service background to form Anchor Network Solutions – with the goal of giving small business owners something they weren't used to: IT consulting and support from people that could speak plain English, communicate effectively, and provide a high level of customer service.

Vince is the CEO of Anchor Network Solutions, a Denver-based Managed IT service provider and technology consulting firm founded in 2002. His firm delivers big business technology on a small business budget and with white glove service to its clients.

A CompTIA Managed Services Trustmark holder, Anchor provides technology consulting services to small and medium-sized businesses in Colorado and around the country. The company is nationally recognized and was ranked #4 on the MSPmentor Small Business 100 IT service provider list and has been featured in *PCWorld, Business Solutions Magazine,* and *The Denver Post* for the service they deliver.

Vince is a frequent presenter at IT conferences, and in recent years has been recognized by MSPmentor and SMB Nation as one of the top small business technology executives, and for his participation and contribution to the SMB IT community.

You can connect with Vince at:
Vince@anchornetworksolutions.com
http://www.linkedin.com/in/vincetinnirello
https://twitter.com/vtinnirello

CHAPTER 14

APPLICATION DEVELOPMENT

BY RAJ KOSURI

Application development within a corporation can be a daunting task and involves a collaborative effort among multiple resources to obtain a successful outcome. Achieving optimum results in High Impact application development means having the right people involved, establishing a high-level design specification, optimizing for business and regulatory compliance, and obtaining stake holder approval. Without these vital four components the plan is likely doomed to failure. However, carefully administrating these factors will greatly enhance the potential for a winning design and implementation.

As of this writing, the country is in the throes of what has become known as the greatest IT-related debacle in the history of the United States Government, that is, healthcare.gov. This is a prime example of a rollout with a good application strategy. There is story after story of the difficulties with this rollout of technology and it has impacted millions of Americans. If you start application development without proper direction by neglecting the four components identified above, the outcome will be disastrous and can costs thousands or millions of dollars to correct as is the case with healthcare.gov. The United States Government wasted approximately $130 Million in development and it is projected that it will take another $300 Million to fix it.

If you do application development correctly from the beginning, you will have a better product. Instead of costing you money, your design can increase your business revenue or at least make your business processes more efficient. Let's break down the four Critical Components of Application Development.

FOUR CRITICAL COMPONENTS OF APPLICATION DEVELOPMENT

1. Get the Right People Involved

- Involve the proper business and IT stakeholders. This must be done from the very beginning. Carefully identify those individuals and make sure they are included. Make sure to get your domain experts involved. You will also want to look for the most talented available resources within your organization and aim to create a multi-disciplinary team that involves architects, testers, IT, BAs, and UX specialists who can help you build your high-level design from multiple perspectives.

- Establish the ground rules for design and align everyone's involvement with business priorities. Whenever possible, avoid conflicts of interest and establish a governance process for reconciling conflicting design approaches.

- Understand your resource constraints and develop mitigation strategies to address those issues.

- After building the high-level project team, clearly define the roles and responsibilities of each member of the team.

- Watch out for:

  - Politics. Domain experts can exert their influence to better their position for high profile projects. Map design to business priorities and KPI to keep the discussions objective.

  - Expectations. Coming in as domain experts, everyone needs to understand that respect will be earned through their own merit in the design process rather than their current title.

- Lack of documentation. Capture all discussion points to have an archive of decisions that led to a choice of suitable designs.

2. Establish a High-Level Design Specification

• Determine the right approach to design creation. At this stage you will be determining what the project is designed to do. What will be the ultimate outcome of your work?

• Understand the design process. For example, if a part of your design will involve ecommerce, you will have to understand where credit card information can be stored and where it cannot be stored. If you store credit card information incorrectly, you will subject your customers to a higher risk of credit card theft and potential negative ramifications to your company.

• Determine the right approach to design documentation and build a high-level design document that illustrates the flow of information through users, processes, applications, and infrastructure.

• Create use cases according to defined business, technical, and functional requirements.

• Build the high-level design. This is like the GPS for your project and will guide your team throughout the life of the application/design process.

  - Build a high-level design document that illustrates the flow of information through users, processes, applications, and infrastructure.

  - Create use cases according to defined business, technical, and functional requirements.

• Specify the impact of the design on other projects.

• Designs can be created in four different ways, depending on the requirements stability and the application complexity:

  - *Just-in-Time (JIT) Design* is best used in an agile setting where the design itself evolves as more information becomes clear during successive iterations.

- *Iterative Design* takes advantage of high requirements stability to progressively enhance design to account for all levels of application complexity.

- *A Prototype Design* is intended to take advantage of low application complexity to rapidly create designs as requirements change.

- *Full Design* is a complete design done in a short timeframe due to low application complexity and well known, stable requirements.

3. Optimize for Business and Regulatory Compliance

• Understand the importance of compliance checks.

• Mitigate the difficulties of managing compliance by:

- Ensuring your high-level design is compliant with the organization's design standards.

- Ensuring your design is in alignment with your business and IT strategy.

- Ensuring compliance with the enterprise architecture, the security plan, and applicable laws, regulations, and contracts. In many industries there are very strict compliance regulations in place, often including significant fines and even potential imprisonment for non-compliance. It is imperative that your application design team fully understands the regulatory aspects of your business and the potential ramifications for non-compliance.

4. Obtain Stakeholder Approval

• Obtain stakeholder approval for the high-level design.

• Ensure all stakeholders are aligned in their understanding of high-level design and requirements. You cannot afford to have any confusion at this level. It is extremely important that everyone is on the same page related to the design. It is important for stakeholders to realize that design is not a zero sum political strategy. Rather, it is about creating win-win solutions that ultimately benefit the organization. It is very likely that some stakeholders will be disappointed with this. The way to handle this is to always point to the overall organizational gain, which ultimately benefits all stakeholders in the long term.

- Ensure stakeholders are kept up to date on the progress of your project. Keeping stakeholders aware of, and involved in, the development process is key to maintaining stakeholder alignment around the final deliverable.

- Stakeholders must be aware that the design will evolve as understanding of the project grows.

FIND THE RIGHT APPROACH TO DESIGN CREATION

Designs can be created in four different ways, depending on the requirements stability and the application complexity:

- *Just-in-Time (JIT) Design* is best used in an agile setting where the design itself evolves as more information becomes clear during successive iterations.

- *Iterative Design* takes advantage of high requirements stability to progressively enhance design to account for all levels of application complexity.

- *A Prototype Design* is intended to take advantage of low application complexity to rapidly create designs as requirements change.

- *Full Design* is a complete design done in a short time frame due to low application complexity and well known, stable requirements.

Let's examine each of these designs in more detail:

A. Just-in-Time (JIT)

What's involved?

- Based on the premise that a full design cannot be implemented up front due to changing business conditions or requirements, a continually-evolving design is necessary.

- Only the most stable requirements are built into the design. As future requirements become more stable, they are incorporated into the design. In this way, the design evolves "just in time" as the requirements are stabilized rather than trying to estimate future requirements.

Pros:

- It reduces the risk of over-engineering to try and accommodate a future requirement that may never materialize.

Cons:

- Future enhancements to design will involve refactoring and possible rework of previous efforts as new requirements are fitted into the evolving architecture

B. Iterative Design

What's involved?

- This approach assumes a stable requirements base. However, these requirements need to be addressed at multiple levels. Each of these levels is exposed in an iteration where additional requirements are accommodated and the design refined accordingly.

Pros:

- It takes account of all requirements before development commences which makes downstream tasks much easier.

- An iterative approach accounts for all stakeholder views with appropriate opportunity to discuss trade-offs early.

Cons:

- It could take time to settle on a suitable design through iteration if the number of stakeholders is large.

- Once the process commences, resource commitment is necessary to avoid losing institutional knowledge from previous iterations.

C. Prototype Design

What's involved?

- With continually changing requirements, it is not possible to stabilize on a given design. It is possible, however, to create conceptual designs that can be used for further discussions.

- Prototype design is useful for initial proof of concepts where all the issues may not be understood. By going through the design exercise, more requirements become apparent and the prototype is discarded for an entirely new design.

Pros:

- It provides flexibility to discard designs early in the process while learning about the solution domain continues to occur.

- Useful for Rapid Application Development (RAD) environments where development is time sensitive.

Cons:

- With a large number of stakeholders, confusion can creep in if the velocity of change is too high. Requirements can sometimes get revisited even though the latest prototype addresses the need.

D. Full Design

What's involved?

- With a sufficiently low complexity application or highly specific problem domain, it is possible to complete the entire design in one pass.

- It assumes all requirements are well known and have been obtained previously.

- All design perspectives are accommodated in the final design prior to release. There are no subsequent iterations.

Pros:

- Can easily integrate in the SDLC as a design phase with a greater degree of accuracy around completion date.

Cons:

- The design assumes stability of third-party integration. If the design of those applications changes, this may trigger a change and shift to an iterative design approach.

WORKING WITH YOUR DESIGN TEAM

Will everything go smoothly in the design process? It is quite unlikely, even when you make every effort to follow the steps I have outlined above. After all, you are still working with people who will inevitably disagree at some point about any number of issues. There are ways to resolve issues and possibly even prevent certain things from arising that could potential derail your project. Below are some potential hazards you may encounter along the way and how you can effectively handle these issues if they should arise.

(i). Process Collision

This is where process owners approach the same problem in different ways. Changing any one of the processes is a difficult task that involves retraining and possible redevelopment with full testing. You can mitigate this problem by resolving the differences between the two processes. If this is unsuccessful, then create a process buffer that accepts both process flows into a third process that feeds the application. It is not efficient, but it is better than the alternative.

(ii). Hostage Taking

This is where a key stakeholder refuses to participate in the project after a certain design stage and the project cannot move forward without their involvement. In this case, escalation to the steering committee is usually necessary to reach a resolution.

(iii). Business-Led Implementation

This is where IT is viewed as a cost center and must do what the business requires. In this scenario, the business leads the design effort through a one sided approach without concern for effort or enterprise optimization. Given the inherent risk in this approach, many decisions may need to be revisited. It is better to take an agile approach with the business setting priorities for each sprint.

(iv). Misalignment of Stakeholder Priorities

This is where each stakeholder has their own agenda without compromise therefore requiring a very complicated design to address all needs. With the risk of cost overrun quite high, the best approach is to use an agile approach.

IT TAKES A TEAM AND A GOOD DESIGN

As Kenneth Lambert said, "A good design is essential to solving any complex problem." This certainly holds true in the design world of application development. Your team is essential to your success and their ability to work collaboratively is imperative. As you work together you will be amazed at the accomplishments that will be achieved.

About Raj

Raj Kosuri deeply believes in "Simple Living & High Thinking" and possesses extraordinary technical expertise in the field of Information Technology and business acumen. He wears a contagious warm smile on his face, which makes others comfortable with him even before he commences an interaction. Being a family man, he loves spending time with his family and ensures he makes quality time for them religiously. He waits to play his favorite soccer game with his 9-year-old son in his indoor make-shift stadium. He strictly likes to keep his official business countenance and his home disposition far away from each other. He has an undying passion for driving from his youth, and is ready to take to wheels any time of the day. This unique mix in his personality has given him the right recipe to build up his IQ and appetite to run and grow business with the right spirit.

Raj believes that sharing knowledge and innovation are among the most effective ways of progressing – especially in the field of Information Technology. As CEO & CTO he has authored *Best Practices for Business Rules Integration* in 2006 to share his expertise with the world. His chapter on Mobile Application is yet another way to do so. He led his company to the "Deloitte Fast 50 & 500" four years in a row. He was awarded the honor of being named one of the **Smart 100 CEOs** by *SmartCEO* Magazine in 2009. In the same year, he introduced "Verdio" the Green PC – which won the **NVTC Green Award** for Small Business 2010. That was not all, in 2011, Raj released the Climetric Software designed to help Fortune 500 companies with carbon management and accounting. Raj has very optimistically developed the Green Data Center in Danville, VA – spread across 27,000 sq feet to offer cloud computing, disaster recovery and business continuity solutions in a virtualized environment. He plans to generate local employment there for those qualified – allowing them to stay in their hometown and work.

CHAPTER 15

CYBER SECURITY

BY CHARLES HENSON

Regardless of size, cyber security protection is essential for any business that relies on the Internet in any capacity to help perform its daily functions. Businesses process payments, collect information, perform research, utilize cloud-based services, and correspond with clients or customers via the Internet. It's a natural fit and the opportunity to maximize business profitability is greater than ever because of the Internet; however, the risk of having some entity wanting access to the information your business has obtained is also great.

One of the largest problems facing business owners today is the risk of cyber security breaches. Fraud is rampant and to make matters more frustrating, there are multiple ways that a business can be attacked. The five most common types of cyber crime are:

- Hacking
- Identity theft
- Malicious software
- Phishing attacks
- Malicious code/website redirects

You may be wondering, "What could my business have that's of value to these criminals?" There's more than what you may realize. Cyber criminals are eager for opportunities to collect bank account numbers, disable your system, obtain your passwords or obtain your customer base that you work with through the Internet. It's a different kind of crime than what we're used to, where someone has to go to a location to see what your business has that they want. Today they can do it all from anywhere in the world as long as they have Internet access. You may feel that your money is safe sitting in the bank's vault, but with cyber crime, criminals can gain access to your money while sitting anywhere in the world.

The great news for business owners is that they can learn from past events and take proactive measures for the future to lessen their chances of being the next cyber victim. Doing this is one of the most effective ways to ensure that your business remains more stable, thus more successful.

TROJANS AND RANSOMWARE

Have you ever heard of a Trojan or ransomware? Many people don't recognize what that is until it's too late and they have an infection running amuck in their computer system. The CryptoLocker is a great example of a ransomware Trojan. It is spread by a malicious attachment or link, usually sent via e-mail attachment, which can spread through a computer network in the blink of an eye. It does a great amount of damage in a very short amount of time. Even a business with sound security measures in place can learn about this the hard way.

One law firm that experienced this was a smaller firm, about seven attorneys, several paralegals, and a few other staff. Someone at the firm had been examining a clients exported e-mail inbox for information on a case—innocent enough. Unfortunately, an attachment in one of the e-mails was an infected file that included the CryptoLocker Trojan, which infiltrated their network system and encrypted their files.

When a file is encrypted it cannot be opened without the encryption key. Obviously, if you didn't put the key on it yourself and no one in your firm did, it's hard to find out what it is and without this encryption key, you can no longer open the file. Furthermore, when you try opening the file it encrypts your other data files and that's when the real havoc begins. Someone else on your network tries to open one of the encrypted files and suddenly everything is locked up as it spreads throughout your network infecting all of your PC's and servers.

While everyone is trying to figure out what's going on a message pops up: "In order to un-encrypt your files, we need you to provide a payment via a pre-paid voucher service and then we will give you the encryption code to un-encrypt your files." This type of an attack is referred to as ransomware. The hackers are holding your files and/or information until you pay a ransom. Then they ask for your credit card information. Some people give it and then they are headed toward identity theft or some surprise charges on that card, plus they still are short an encryption code because the hackers never intended to give back access to their data. The hackers only wanted to gain access to their money and credit card information. For this firm, it didn't happen because they didn't try paying the ransom, but if they DID try to pay ransom it would have led to more issues.

The challenging part about this is that you cannot keep it secret. The firm got my IT Company in there quickly to resolve their significant problem. Plus, they had to scramble around to reschedule court dates and explain to clients, judges, and associates in a very professional way what had happened. Aside from the stress and anxiety of the CryptoLocker attack for the business, there could have been other potential or undesirable side effects, including: research and information gone if it was done after the last back-up, negative repercussions with clients, and possible data breaches. Thankfully, this firm did not have that concern. They were fortunate because my firm was able to restore data from their managed backup system and my engineers were very thorough in getting their systems clean.

In summary, it becomes quite a major public relations issue when you have a cyber attack and the clean-up of the computers may take three days—exponentially more depending on the size of business—but the effects can be longer term.

Of course, we don't want business owners to be frightened. The Internet provides as many benefits to business as it does risks. The key is to put yourself in a position where you maximize your security. When you do that everyone wins and business can carry on as usual.

SEVEN WAYS TO BEEF UP YOUR CYBER SECURITY

Hackers may work overtime to try and cause trouble for business owners, but the "good guys," the ones who want your business to operate smoothly, efficiently and securely have come up with some highly effective ways to help protect the information that you have on your server. These seven ways to enhance your cyber security should be considered by all business owners, as they are a safeguard to better business practices.

1) <u>Anti-virus protection:</u> There are two ways that you can have anti-virus protection for a computer network. You can either have an active subscription or pay a monitoring fee (usually monthly). There are many IT companies out there that serve clients who own businesses and help them monitor the activity that is taking place proactively, thereby reducing their chances of getting infected by a virus. Regardless of which route you go, it is important to have current anti-virus protection.

2) <u>Anti-malware protection:</u> Malware is malicious software that gets installed on your computer with or without your knowledge. It usually happens by clicking on a malicious e-mail link or by browsing a website that has been infected. The malware resides "in the background" of your computer and does malicious things—just as its name implies. Malware and spyware begin to watch where you're going when you are online and what you are searching for. For example, if you are looking for comforters you may start seeing ads everywhere about comforters. This can be both overwhelming and annoying, but it is a sure sign that some sort of malware is on a computer.

3) <u>Managed firewall with content filtering:</u> With this protection feature, you can see which users in your business are browsing the Internet and what sites they are visiting. You can decide the types of websites that are inappropriate for viewing during company work hours and the firewall can block

those types of sites from being viewed from your businesses network. One additional element to this that is important and recommended by all businesses is to implement an Internet usage policy. This policy will clearly define what sites you allow your employees to visit and what types of browsing activities they are allowed to do on the business computers.

4) <u>Domain Naming Service Routing</u>: A great way to help reduce the risk of getting your PC infected is to redirect all of your Internet traffic through a Direct Name Server (DNS) router software. The way this works is that when you try to go to a specific website your computer, using this software, finds the IP address, translates it, and then takes you directly to that website. It allows all traffic through a secure server so you know that when you try to go someplace in specific, you end up there and not at some malicious site that may be sitting there, waiting to answer your request. DNS router software also gives alerts and blocks places that you don't want to go, helping ensure potential attacks are reduced.

5) <u>Secure E-mail and SPAM Protection</u>: Employees need to be educated on e-mail safety so they can identify the signs of what may be a malicious e-mail. Using anti-spam filtering software allows you to filter all e-mails that come into your business server and have them inspected for any malicious properties. If a "suspect" e-mail comes through it will strip out the file and keep the e-mail protected. In the event that a virus type attachment does make it through the anti-spam screening, it is essential to educate your employees/staff on the dangers of opening such types of attachments from unknown sources or that seem suspicious. If your users are in doubt, call the sender to confirm they actually sent the e-mail.

6) <u>Back up your data frequently</u>: Many businesses believe that their data is being backed up more than it actually is. Make sure you know exactly how often your data is being backed up and do not take anything for granted. You know that it is being backed up when you either hire someone to manage

it for you, or you review your logs and verify daily that it is being backed up. You should perform a test restore to ensure this is taking place at least once a month but preferably more often. How often should you back up your data? Hourly if possible.

7) <u>Proactive monitoring and patch management:</u> Cyber attacks are also created around vulnerabilities and holes in software. Today there are numerous software applications that are required to efficiently run your business. With this, it is of the upmost importance to ensure you have updated all of your software with the latest patches and updates. Since the hackers are looking at Microsoft, Adobe and other software providers to learn what their latest flaw is, they use these flaws to infect systems. You should run updates on all of your software programs as they become available. If you don't have time to do this, consider hiring an IT firm that offers Managed Services and let them do the updating for you.

These seven ways to increase a business's cyber security are an important aspect of safe business practices and should be followed by all businesses—small, medium, or large. Doing so will help business owners maintain the edge over the potential threats that come with conducting any portion of their business over the Internet or by using the Internet in any capacity.

WORDS TO LIVE BY IN THE CYBER WORLD

Informed business owners will be able to maintain the edge over hackers and other cyber criminals with a combination of knowledge and application. The people who have bad intents for your business have a full time job trying to break into your systems. It is their #1 goal to compromise your system for their malicious good. Your business may be closed for the day but theirs is not.

The problem we see is that many businesses don't think they are important or realize they are a target. In this day and age, everyone with a computer, tablet, smart phone or any device connected to the

Internet is a target. They can all be compromised. That means there is a demand for business owners to protect their property—data, technology, etc.— educate their employees about what is expected of them in this cyber world and know what to look for, in order to keep business running optimally and without interruption due to a cyber breach.

Some cyber criminals may want access to personal data, while others really just want to use your computer system as a means for their automated program to run without end user input. Doing so will inflict damage on others through your computer network and never have it be traced back to them. This may seem like a lot to manage but with the proper consultations and giving serious consideration to hiring an IT firm to manage your business network, you greatly increase your odds of keeping every day a "business as usual" day.

About Charles

Charles Henson has been in the IT industry for over twenty years, getting his first "computer" around 1984 from a school friend. An immediate thought came to mind: if computers break, someone will need to fix them. This simple idea drove Charles to receive his Associates degree in Electrical Engineering from ITT Technical Institute.

Currently serving as Managing Partner for Nashville Computer, Charles started working for the growing firm in 1991. In May 2010, he was invited to the Google Headquarters in California for his personal feedback on Google products. Charles has been interviewed and featured in *Redmond IT* magazine regarding Backup Disaster Recovery solutions. He has worked with and has been trained on Public Key Infrastructure (PKI), a technology used to encrypt data and communications. Each week he leads discussion groups of IT leaders around the country, comparing notes and staying on top of technology problems, changes, and trends.

Charles is passionate about helping business owners and office staffs become well educated about all of the technologies that can help them grow, be more efficient, and stay safe dealing with today's cyber security issues. He feels it is his job to become a trusted advisor to all who will benefit from his IT experience and has become well known around the Nashville area through speaking engagements at seminars, giving interviews to news reporters, and hosting tele-seminars and webinars. He has also written two books, *Hassle-Free Computer Support* and *Cloud Computing: A Guide for Executives & Business Owners*.

Charles currently lives in Brentwood, Tennessee with his wife of more than twenty years and their two children. Charles often tells his potential clients, "I am local and you may run into me in the store, in the park, or while out with the family."

CHAPTER 16

THE COST OF IT

BY SCOTT BECK

For most business owners connecting the dots when it comes to technology can be confusing, time consuming, frustrating, and COSTLY! Despite most businesses now relying on technology to operate, many owners continue to ignore their IT until a major issue occurs, resulting in expensive downtime, lost production, idle staff, possible loss of business reputation, and big repair bills.

There are three basic truths concerning IT from the perspective of most business owners:

1) It's confusing, demoralizing, and stressful.

2) It's one of their least favorite aspects of running their business.

3) It's perceived as an expense instead of an investment.

Business owners aren't sure what they should be paying for IT, how to use IT to streamline operations and increase profitability, or why they keep having ongoing technology problems. Or maybe they have been lucky so far and haven't had any major, budget crushing IT problems, so why sweat it? The unfortunate part is the less attention spent on technology the greater the odds are that something WILL go wrong, usually at the worst possible time!

According to Forrester Research, Inc, in most industries, companies should be spending between 4% – 8% of gross revenues on Information Technology costs. If you are under-spending you are exposing your company to higher risk and you may be missing out on a competitive advantage that your competition is enjoying.

IT BROKE...COME FIX IT

Traditionally, IT support has been delivered in a "Break/Fix" model. You have a computer glitch, pick up the phone and call the computer guy. He fits you into his schedule, comes out and fixes the immediate problem, and sends you a bill for his time.

Here's the problem...The IT industry isn't regulated. There are no accrediting agencies so anyone can open shop and call themselves an "expert," even if they have no formal training or industry certifications. There is no black book defining service rates or what average repair times should be.

There is a fundamental conflict of interest between you and your support provider. Being paid by the hour, there are no incentives for them to actually stabilize your computer network or quickly resolve problems. This means all the risks are shifted to YOU for things like unforeseen circumstances, scope creep, or learning curve inefficiencies. Essentially, the more problems you have, the more they profit.

Second, it creates a management problem for you. Now you have to try and keep track of the hours they've worked to ensure you aren't getting overbilled; and since you often have no way of really knowing the actual amount of hours worked, it creates a situation where you really need to be able to trust they are 100% ethical and honest AND tracking THEIR hours properly (not all do).

Lastly, it makes budgeting for technology expenses a nightmare – since they may be zero one month and thousands the next.

SUPPORT 2.0...BETTER, STRONGER, FASTER

Technology Management (or Managed Services) allows the business owner and IT Support Company to focus on the same goals and objectives: helping your business run faster, easier, and more profitably.

Think of a property management firm. Tenants pay them a fixed monthly fee and they take care of maintaining the grounds, snow removal, property taxes, perform building maintenance, dealing with any building repairs, and coordinate working with the trades on any plumbing and electrical needs. It's the same concept with technology.

Plus, the more your provider can automate maintenance, build efficiency of service, lower your business risks, and lower the amount of technology issues your staff experience, the more profitable your business is (less system downtime, more efficient staff, increased productivity and production, etc.) and the more profitable the relationship is for the provider (less time fixing issues equals higher profit margins). It's now in both of your interests to ensure the technology "just works."

HIDDEN COSTS AND OTHER GOTCHAS

Unfortunately not all IT support providers or Technology Management agreements are created equally. It may be tempting to choose the lowest cost option, however, these can end up costing WAY more. If the monthly fee is clearly way lower than your area's normal average, then alarm bells should go off. It could signify the company is a startup learning off your dime, lacks experience in the field, or is moonlighting from their full time IT job. Who will they prioritize when push comes to shove, their full time job or responding to your issues? A steady paycheck is going to win every time!

Be mindful of any small print and other hidden gotchas. Always make sure that "what is and isn't included" is CLEARLY defined. Be careful of long term – two, three, or more year – agreements and know their associated penalties for cancelling the agreement early.

LEARN FROM OTHERS

Ask any IT professional, "What's the worst that can happen?" and you might be shocked and dismayed at what they have seen and the impact it had on businesses.

Can you imagine losing the ability to contact your clients by email?

Or worse yet, being told by your Internet Service Provider (ISP) that your location has been blasting out thousands of spam email with viruses and you need to fix the issue within 48 hours or lose your Internet connection? Either of these scenarios in this day and age would certainly cripple most business operations. Imagine having both happen at the same time!

This was the exact scenario a business was faced with. They attempted to fix the issue themselves, without success, after their Internet provider advised them of the problem. Then came the 48-hours–or-else warning. Realizing they were in over their heads, they reached out for help.

Long story short, investigating the problem we discovered the computers hadn't been updated in ages, there was a mix and match of anti-virus software (some systems even had expired anti-virus versions), no malware protection, were using a router designed for home use that lacked business level protections, and there was a lack of any monitoring of network traffic.

This allowed a virus to enter their network and spread amongst their computers. As systems got infected they became email spam bots— sending out hundreds of virus infected emails every hour to clients, personal, and random email addresses. These outgoing emails lead to the company getting placed on an Internet Spam Blacklist.

Imagine sending a letter out in the mail and the postal service returning it as undeliverable. As the client attempted to send legitimate emails to their clients, those using these Blacklists as part of their spam protection refused their emails; effectively making it impossible for them to communicate by email with their clients.

It took many hours to clean the infections, update the computers, stabilize the network, and jump through the hoops to get them off the Blacklist so their email could flow again.

Factoring in the cost or repair, idle staff time, lost production, and estimating the cost to their business reputation, this one event easily cost them about a half years' worth of what it would have cost to have a Technology Management plan in place that would have helped avoid the hassle and frustrations in the first place.

Another business had installed an expensive tape backup system. For two years the daily reports said everything was working, however, the backups were never actually checked to ensure data WAS recoverable. You guessed it, when they had an urgent need to recover data, the system hadn't worked in months and the data wasn't available. We were able to eventually recover the data for them with the help of an expensive high end data recovery company. The time to conduct a fire drill isn't during a fire, yet time and again we see businesses that lack both local and offsite backups and have no testing regime to ensure the data IS recoverable.

Preventing technology problems and keeping your systems up and running (which is what Technology Management services is all about), is a LOT less expensive and damaging to your organization than waiting until a major problem occurs and then paying for emergency IT support to restore your systems to working order.

THREE TIPS FOR DRIVING DOWN YOUR IT COSTS

If your biggest business cost is like most companies, it's employees. The quickest and easiest way to improve the bottom line is to ensure staff has the ability to work efficiently and ensuring you minimize lost productivity costs.

1) *Stop Reacting and Get Proactive.* Think of your vehicle. It's recommended that you change the oil, flush the radiator, replace fuel filters, and the list goes on. We COULD choose to skip the maintenance, however, we know if we do, the vehicle WILL eventually break down and it'll likely happen when we are in a rush. Once the vehicle is stuck on the side of the road, we also know it's going to cost more to fix it. The tow truck, more complex repairs, longer time without its use, rental car expense. So it goes with your computers and business network. Don't wait for problems to occur, try and avoid them!

2) *Implement a Web Filtering Strategy.* Many businesses are unknowingly providing their staff a $2,000 to $7,000 bonus each year. Studies have shown it's not uncommon for employees to spend several hours each day surfing the Internet for personal use…checking personal email, Facebook, YouTube, Twitter, personal banking, instant messaging, online shopping, downloading media. The temptations are practically limitless.

If an employee is averaging two hours a day on the web for personal use, that's ten hours a week, forty hours each month, or four hundred eighty hours yearly. If they make $15/hour that's a loss of $7,200/year! Even if it's only one hour a day, that's still $3,600 per employee on average. It doesn't take long for personal web use on the company dime to quickly turn into a large chunk of change. Just think, it only takes ten minutes an hour to start adding up to over an hour of work lost each day!

3) *Use Dual Monitors.* Several studies have shown this simple concept can increase bottom line productivity by as much as 30%. If an employee's duties are tied directly to using a computer there's a good chance they spend most of the day minimizing and maximizing windows as they switch between programs (email, Excel, Word, etc.) Plus, if they need to compare documents they have to print off one version (wasted paper and toner) to compare against the version on the screen. Having dual monitors allows having multiple windows open at once and maximizes what can be quickly viewed.

ASK BETTER QUESTIONS

Often business owners will ask, "What does it cost?" when they really should be asking, "What am I getting for my money?" Many hours go into building the process, procedures, and policies to assist owners in maximizing performance, lowering risks, and getting predictable results from their IT investments.

For example, on average, it takes an hour every month to proactively maintain a computer; additional time for servers. Then there are the system logs to be reviewed for any brewing issues, test backup recoveries to be performed, security access logs checked, anti-virus and malware scan results to be reviewed, software updates to be approved and installed. The list goes on. Then there is a huge investment in software and hardware used to deliver the services, the ongoing staff training, error and omissions insurance, actual office space, service vehicle expenses, etc.

While it might be possible for a company to obtain the software most Technology Management companies utilize, the cost of implementing, learning, maintaining, and operating them tends to be cost prohibitive and distracts resources from their primary job functions. IT Professionals will already know the research and development of new products or services that will further help their clients streamline operations and build efficiencies.

By leveraging a reputable Technology Management firm, a company is getting the knowledge and experience they bring to the table. Because these firms have multiple clients they are exposed to more situations and can help you avoid costly mistakes made by others or offer ways to improve how things are being done – based on the results other clients enjoy.

About Scott

Scott Beck's journey into technology started in 1993 while employed as an On-Air Radio Personality. The station he was at became the first in Atlantic Canada to implement a "Live Assist" computer system that controlled what played on the air and eventually led to the downsizing of staff. Surviving the cuts, he decided the best job security was to learn about computers!

In the following years, his "Computer Hobby" developed into a true passion. Leaving his position with the Department of Justice Canada, where he had been exposed to networks and servers, he returned to school to become Industry Certified. Graduating Top 7 from a two-year program, which he completed in just one year, Scott earned several certifications: Microsoft Certified Systems Engineer, Cisco Certified Network Associate, CompTIA Network+ and CompTIA A+.

In 2002, Scott started asking small business owners and executives what they disliked about their computers, network and support. Over and over again, he heard spine-tingling, blow-by-blow accounts of things like:

- Our computer people take days to return my calls ... and when they do, all I hear is finger-pointing. Isn't anyone accountable for anything anymore?

- It's too complicated...we just want to do our jobs, run our business...

- Nobody understands how it impacts my business when things don't run properly.

- I spend all this money on equipment and see no returns on the investment... They didn't even explain why I needed the new stuff or what it was going to do for my business.

- What time is it? It's got to be getting close to lunchtime. My computer's already locked up at least twice today.

- What am I paying for? Their bill and explanations are always in Geek Speak.

Seeing an opportunity to provide something different, BeckTek—a Technology Management Firm—was launched in March 2004 to help small businesses owners and executives run their businesses faster, easier and more profitably.

Protecting clients' best interests and delivering a superior client service experience earned BeckTek a coveted Greater Moncton Excellence Award for Service Excellence, the only IT Company to do so in the twenty-seven year history of the awards. In 2014, BeckTek received a Moncton Times & Transcript Reader's Choice Award.

Since opening BeckTek, Scott has talked before, met with and worked with, hundreds of business owners and executives throughout Atlantic Canada. Scott enjoys helping business professionals get past their fears and uncertainty regarding technology. He is passionate about reducing client's business risks, turning technology into a competitive advantage, and improving their profitability.

CHAPTER 17

SERVICE DESK

BY DEBBIE ASKIN

Most business owners, company employees and Information Technology (IT) professionals would agree that their company's IT Service Desk is one of the most important functions that keep their systems running day-in and day-out. After all, the IT Service Desk is usually the end-user's main contact with their IT organization. When there is a problem, the end-user wants to be able to pick up the telephone and place a call directly to a live person who will be able to help them resolve their immediate IT issue during the call. The experience a user has with the Service Desk creates their overall perception of the IT Department. This is where customer satisfaction begins (and often ends). Because of the significance of this role, it is imperative to have the right people in these positions who have the training and experience to provide first call resolution to the caller's problem whenever possible.

An IT Service Desk (or sometimes referred to as a "Help Desk") can add enormous value to any business by identifying and resolving IT issues quickly and efficiently, therefore keeping all employees working and thus saving the company countless man hours as well as contributing to the overall efficiency of the organization. The overall goal of any Service Desk should be to provide a single integrated solution to manage incidents, issues or problems for the end user – while also tracking the same to create a repeatable system of problem solving.

AN IMPORTANT DECISION: HIRE OR OUTSOURCE MY SERVICE DESK?

Over the last 10 years, I have observed the trend for businesses to decide to outsource their Service Desk responsibilities. They outsource for a number of reasons including the following:

- Access to more diverse personnel with focused knowledge and expertise.

- Enable the business to focus internal resources on their core competencies.

- Staff who are continuously trained in the most up-to-date industry best practices.

- Provide better service levels than trying to create an internally-staffed IT Service Desk.

- A well-staffed service desk can easily respond to spikes in call volume.

- Cost Reduction. Outsourcing should be cheaper than hiring.

- Business Continuity and Availability from redundant systems and generator powered facilities.

Team Askin Technologies, Inc. (TATI) began as a software development company in 1992. As TATI's projects moved into production, the company naturally provided Tier 3 application support. It quickly became evident to company CEO Debbie Askin that Tier 1 service desk capabilities were severely lacking in many of the organizations based upon the kinds of calls that were being escalated to Tier 3. She then set about to build a better service desk based upon ISO and ITIL principles which lead to TATI winning its first service desk contract in 2007. Since then TATI has continued to refine its service delivery model and is actively engaged in bringing the service desk practice to a wide audience in both the commercial and government sectors.

Being our own Service Desk provider has allowed us to see firsthand the benefits of Service Desk outsourcing. We handle everything from ticket creation for incidents and service requests to change and configuration management. End users contacting the service desk do not know that we are not sitting in the companies' own office because we answer each call with a personalized script.

We have equipped our 15,000 sq. ft. facility with four configurable service desk areas to provide security to our clients. We have fully redundant power and communications capabilities allowing us to provide uninterrupted 24/7/365 availability to our customers.

A common question that comes up in conversations with small businesses is, "How do I choose a Service Desk provider?" That is a very legitimate question when you realize there are such a wide variety of interpretations of "Service" in the Service Desk outsourcing environment. As with any niche industry, there will be those companies that do as little as possible to get by and then there will be others that will continuously strive to exceed the expectations of their customers. Of course, everyone else is scattered throughout those two ends of the Service Desk spectrum. But, to address this question, let's examine some fundamental criteria to be considered when searching for a qualified Service Desk provider.

SIX IMPORTANT CONSIDERATIONS WHEN SELECTING A SERVICE DESK PROVIDER

1. Experience

How long a company has been providing Service Desk services is very important for two reasons. First, it tells you they have been in the business for an extended period of time enabling them to grow and evolve into a strong entity that will be able to serve you well. Second, their years of experience speaks to their staying power. You don't want to hassle your employees with switching providers every 6 months. If a company has at least 5 years of experience, it is likely they will continue to be in business for years to come. The last thing you need is to contract with a Service Desk provider only to have them close their doors after a short duration. Finally, request a list of their references. If they lack glowing references that speak to their ability to easily handle whatever your company can throw at them, then find another provider.

2. Cost Effectiveness

One of the important driving factors in seeking to outsource the Service Desk responsibilities is based on saving money, and each business must do their proper due diligence to evaluate this option for themselves. Many companies will claim that they are saving you money, but you really have to evaluate everything that they are providing and compare it against an in-house resource. My experience has been that outsourcing can be a very cost-effective solution allowing companies to become more profitable and effective in delivering the services in which they excel. You want to look for savings of at least 30% compared to the cost of staffing an in-house Service Desk. Be careful in your analysis to compare similar services and service levels, as many companies will attempt to bundle in additional services (at an added cost) or provide you a super low rate for their services, with an unacceptable guaranteed response rate and level of service.

3. Certifications and Training

International Standards bring technological, economic and societal benefits. They help to harmonize technical specifications of products and services making industry more efficient and breaking down barriers to international trade. Organizations and companies often want to get certified to ISO's management system standards (for example ISO 9001, ISO 20000 or ISO 27001) although certification is not a requirement. The best reason for wanting to implement these standards is to improve the efficiency and effectiveness of the company operations.

Each standard supports its own benefits within every industry. however, the common benefits across the certifications include: widened market potential, compliance to procurement tenders, improved efficiency and cost savings, higher level of customer service, and therefore satisfaction, and heightened staff morale and motivation. By having a recognized management standard, it tells your customers that you are serious about their needs.

A serious Service Desk provider will have invested the time and energy in becoming ISO 20000 certified. This is a rigorous process and those holding this designation are among the best in the business. The standard requires annual audits by outside parties to ensure compliance. Additionally, the Service Desk provider should demonstrate exactly how they keep their representatives abreast of all new trends and advancements in their industry.

The Service Desk provider should assure that all technical team members are ITIL certified. ITIL provides the industry best practice guidelines for delivering IT services. This education enables the representatives to perform their job with a higher level of expertise and with the ability to appropriately respond to their customer, determine the proper avenue to take based on the information supplied by the customer, and then take the appropriate action to resolve the issue.

The Microsoft Office Specialist (MOS) designation should also be a minimum requirement for the staff of the Service Desk provider. Through this education they will have a thorough knowledge of the products that 99.9% of the industry uses.

The bottom line in regard to certification and training is that the Service Desk provider and their staff must be appropriately trained and certified to be able to provide the professional service that would be anticipated and expected by their customers. They must know what they are doing! Their training must be thorough and consistent.

4. Contingency Plan and Location

Your Service Desk must be available when you need them. Your Service Desk must be available even if they experience a catastrophic event at their physical location. Be sure to review any prospective provider's written contingency plan before hiring them so that you have assurance of their stability.

A few years ago in our part of the country we experienced what came to be known as "Snowmageddon." It was so extreme that even the federal government in Washington DC was closed for a week. Although we were in the midst of the same catastrophic weather, we were able to continue providing our Service Desk operations, working remotely as needed; we had several feet of snow on the ground. Because of our technological infrastructure and the generator backup in our service center, we were able to continue to function as normal with staff working in the office and remotely. We continued to be fully staffed in spite of the conditions and we were able to service all of our customers from the West Coast to Washington, DC.

Our staff is equipped with the necessary equipment to be able to work remotely at a moment's notice, if necessary. We also have contingency offsite locations established over the entire country, which enable us to continue to be functional in case our facility becomes non-functional for any reason. These locations are available to us and not only provide us with physical working space, but also accommodate our staff for extended stays if necessary.

This is the type of contingency plan your Service Desk provider should have in place in case of a catastrophic event. It is important for the Service Desk customer to know that they can have full confidence that their Service Desk will be available to them at all times because they have the correct infrastructure in place to allow for immediate remote functionality and relocation if necessary.

5. Industry Best Practices and Service Level Agreements (SLA)

What Industry Best Practices are being utilized by your Service Desk provider? These practices will be identified in their Service Level Agreement or SLA. An SLA is a document that outlines in detail what the customer should expect from their Service Desk.

Minimum criteria you should be looking for in the SLA include the following:

- First Call Resolution – Above 85% and preferably closer to 95%.

- Dropped Call Rate – How many people hang up before they speak to an agent.

- Time to Answer - Less than 30 seconds and preferably less than 15 seconds.

- Average Hold Time – How long are people kept on hold before they are helped.

• Customer Satisfaction – Above 90%.

The Service Desk provider can provide you with all their Best Practices details and information. They should readily offer you these reports, but if not, don't hesitate to ask for them. All of this information is continuously tracked and should be available for your review at least on a monthly basis. If a prospective Service Desk provider is not able to give you these details during the sales process, then don't expect for them to ever be able to provide them to you.

6. Repeatable Processes

For any provider to service their clients in a cost effective manner, they need to train their people to follow specific processes in how to answer each call and ask the right questions to get the appropriate information required to troubleshoot the issue. Many times the user doesn't know what they don't know. They just know something is not working properly and you have to go from there.

To enable my company's Service Desk personnel to handle each call with consistency, we have a library of knowledge-based articles. When we troubleshoot a problem, we have a standard diagnostic script we use to evaluate the issue in the most efficient and expedient way possible. By standardizing "Repeatable Processes" we eliminate the possibility of one agent troubleshooting one way and another agent doing it another way. The accumulation of experience dealing with a single issue allows us to know the most effective way to troubleshoot that issue and resolve the problem quickly. We standardize the way we collect information from the customer, how we process that information and how we use that information to resolve future problems.

Another important part of having a Repeatable Processes strategy is that it gives us the ability to provide accurate reporting to customers. With a standardized process in place, your Service Desk provider can identify very specific recurring problems within your IT infrastructure. It elevates issues that the customer didn't even know they had, via reporting, that summarizes a specific list of data because it was collected in a consistent manner.

It takes time, effort and training to teach your staff to do the same thing all the time. If your Service Desk has a process that says when situation 'A' happens, the technical staff member needs to check documents 'B', 'C' and 'D' before taking any action, then everyone follows the same protocol. If they don't do that, they could be causing bigger problems because they are circumventing the proven workflow process.

CHOOSE YOUR SERVICE DESK PROVIDER WISELY

There are great benefits to partnering with a qualified and experienced Service Desk provider. However, these benefits will only be realized if the right resource is chosen from among the many options available to you. You must first be able to understand and articulate your specific needs and perform a cost and efficiency analysis to determine if outsourcing is the best fit for your situation. Once that has been determined, you should be prepared to take the time to evaluate the right partner by asking the right questions. The information outlined above should enable you to formulate the necessary questions to aid you in the interview process. Keep in mind that not all Service Desk providers are created equal. There will be many that may not be able to meet the standards you require. But be assured, there are qualified resources that function at the highest standards that have the ability to exceed your expectations. And when you find that right resource, cost savings, company efficiency and happy employees will all be yours.

About Debbie

Debbie Askin founded Team Askin Technologies, Inc. in 1992. Debbie has over 23 years experience in the IT industry, with 20 years in management positions. Her experience has spanned projects in finance, service desk, imaging, security, and regulatory technology domains.

With the expansion of the company, Debbie's role has transformed from the hands-on design of mission-critical systems to a business leader dedicated to sound business processes and long term success. Debbie attended George Mason University with a concentration in Computer Science.